LEAVING TRAINS
with BLOOD CIRCUS and NIRVANA · SATURDAY, JULY 23
CENTRAL TAVERN

NIRVANA
BREEDERS
MELVINS
SAT DEC 15 7:30PM
DENVER COLISEUM
ALL AGES SHOW

NIRVANA
TAD
WEDNESDAY
FEBRUARY

NIRVANA
FRI JAN 24 · PHOENECIAN CLUB · SYDNEY

NIRVANA
SAT.MARCH2ND
SPECIAL GUESTS
ANXIETY PROPHETS
AT THE ZOO
1124 FRONT STREET

SONIC YOUTH
27.8.
BREMEN-HEMELINGEN · ALADIN

Nirvana Girl
SUB POP
NIRVANA
THURS. JUNE 22
-COVERED WAGON-

WAH WAH NIGHT CONTINUES WITH
THE FLAMING LIPS
STEEL POLE BATH TUB
NIRVANA
Tues. · Oct. 3 · Blind Pig

SKIN YARD
GIRL TROUBLE
THE FLUID
NIRVANA
FEBRUARY 25 8:30PM
FOUR MORE BANDS
FOUR MORE BUCKS
HUB EAST BALLROOM

NIRVANA
NEVERMIND

NIRVANA
WITH SISTER DOUBLE HAPPINESS
SUNDAY OCTOBER 20

DINOSAUR Jr
SPECIAL GUEST
NIRVANA
HOLLYWOOD PALLADIUM
FRIDAY JUNE 14

NIRVANA/TREE HOUSE
April 1 8 pm

FRIDAY FEBRUARY 16
TAD
NIRVANA
HAYWIRE

MELVINS, NIRVANA AND MACHINE IN TACOMA
$7.00
THE 20TH AT LEGENDS
13th AND FAWCET

COME AND GET IT !......
TAD
NIRVANA
CATERPY
RIVERSIDE

1989. NOVEMBER 21.
KEDD 19 óra
TAD
(usa)
Nirvana
Love
SUB POP
A BOOM!! és a Heavy Metal Klub
közös rendezvénye

NIRVANA
27 DEVILS
JUNE 27

SKIN YARD
COFFIN BREAK
NIRVANA
NOV. 23
SPEEDY O'TUBBS

NIRVANA
Tuesday Oct 19th
$18.50
ALBUQUERQUE
CONVENTION

GREEN DAY: DOOKIE
NIRVANA: NEVERMIND
GREEN DAY
NIRVANA
NEVERMIND
SCHOOL OF ROCK
DOYLESTOWN

SON OF isMaEl
BLISS
INSPECTOR
TV and ride me babies

Nirvana
UTERO
SOUP

NIRVANA
LIVE
FEB 22

PUKKELPOP
SUNDAY 25th AUGUST 1991
KIEWIT HASSELT (B)
LIMBOMANIACS
RID
AN EMOTIONAL FISH
DINOSAUR JR
HOUSE OF LOVE
SONIC YOUTH
THE POGUES
THE RAMONES

the MASQUERADE
Heaven showcase
THE RAMONES
LIFE AND DEATH
EXCEL
ALL
BIG DRILL CAR
BABES IN TOYLAND

NIRVANA
HITTING BIRTH
CAUSTIC SODA
THRILL HAMMER
ROGERNUSIC
FREE CHAMPAIGNE
NEW YEARS EVE
SATYRICON

NIRVANA
JUEVES 2 JULIO 1992 22.30 h.
PLAZA DE TOROS DE VALENCIA

SUB-POP RECORDING ARTISTS
NIRVANA
AND TAD
WITH SPECIAL GUESTS
MON 12th FEB
Thornacopia
SPECIAL EARLY SHOW! STARTS AT 8:30
CATTLE CLUB

WAH-WAH NIGHT CONTINUES WITH
NIRVANA
TAD
AND SPECIAL GUESTS
VICTIM'S FAMILY
APRIL 10 Blind Pig

NIRVANA
SECOND SHOW ADDED!
BUTTHOLE SURFERS
TAD
and M.C. BOBCAT GOLDTHWAIT
Monday January 3
P.N.E. Forum · 7:30 p.m.

NIRVANA
BUTTHOLE SURFERS
CHOKEBORE

NIRVANA
LUSH
KING KRAB

ASUW Productions Presents
NIRVANA
TAD GITS
with CRUNCHBIRD
Saturday, January 6, 1990 8pm.
HUB East Ballroom
University of Washington
FOUR BANDS.
FOUR BUCKS.

NIRVANA
GUEST : THE BUZZCOCKS
L'EVENEMENT
No 3264

NIRVANA
IGUANAS SAT. FEB. 17 also NIRVANA TAD IN HERE

HALLOWEEN Party
B★★★HOLE SURFERS
NIRVANA
BLOOD CIRCUS
FRI- OCT. 28 8PM
UNION STATION
4TH & JACKSON

NOBODY IN PARTICULAR PRESENTS
NIRVANA
BREEDERS
MELVINS
SAT DEC 15 7:30PM
DENVER COLISEUM
ALL AGES SHOW

NIRVANA
THE BREEDERS
IN CONCERT!
FRIDAY, DEC. 3 8:00 P.M.
U.N.O. LAKEFRONT ARENA

NIRVANA
$8
FITS OF DEPRESSION
BIKINI KILL
WED APRIL 17
OK HOTEL
212 ALASKAN WY. PH. 621-7903

NIRVANA
MELVINS
BLOOD MEN
SATYRICON
FRI JAN 12

KURT COBAIN AND NIRVANA

THE COMPLETE ILLUSTRATED HISTORY

WITH
ANDREW EARLES
CHARLES R. CROSS
GILLIAN G. GAAR
BOB GENDRON
TODD MARTENS
MARK YARM

AND
JIM DEROGATIS
ALAN DI PERNA
GREG KOT

WITH PHOTOGRAPHS BY
CHARLES PETERSON
KEVIN ESTRADA
JAY BLAKESBERG
ED SIRRS
IAN TILTON
STEVE DOUBLE

chartwell
books

CONTENTS

1.

GOTTA FIND A WAY
THE PRE-*BLEACH* YEARS

By Charles R. Cross

DRUMMER WANTED. Play hard. sometimes light. underground. versatile. fast. medium. slow. versatile. serious. heavy. versatile. dorky. nirvana. hungry. Kurdt 352-0992.

One of the famous ads run in Seattle's *The Rocket* alternative newspaper during 1987 and 1988 by the duo of Kurt Cobain and Krist Novoselic seeking a drummer.

Though Kurt Cobain will forever be associated with Seattle and the rise of that city's grunge music scene, he actually lived in Seattle for less than two years. During that time he mostly stayed in rentals or hotels, and he didn't own a house there until January 1994, three months before his suicide. He was just twenty-seven when he died above the garage of his newly purchased mansion. When the police searched that Seattle home after his death, they found a basement full of unpacked moving boxes.

Cobain's suicide on April 5, 1994, was tragic, but his artistic accomplishments, particularly in light of his childhood and where he came from, were remarkable by any imagination. Few rock stars have ever risen from such unlikely origins to such heights of fame, and few of any background have created a body of work with such lasting impact on music.

Cobain was born in Aberdeen, Washington, and he spent the first two-thirds of his life in or near the small city of sixteen thousand. To understand Cobain—his roots, the formation of his creative drive, and the genesis of Nirvana—you must understand Aberdeen, and how that city profoundly shaped its most famous son.

Greetings from Aberdeen, Washington.

Though Aberdeen is only two hours west of Seattle, it is an entirely different world in terms of economic opportunity and even landscape. Located in Grays Harbor County, near the rugged and heavily forested Washington coast, Aberdeen came into being to service men harvesting natural resources from the region. In Aberdeen's case, that meant fishing, mining, and logging, and those workers rolled into the city to buy supplies, but also to drink, fight, and, often, whore.

In 1952, *Look* magazine called Aberdeen "one of the hot spots in America's battle against sin" because of the many brothels that lined the downtown streets. A notorious madam named Nellie Curtis was one of the town's colorful characters, said to have more political power than most elected leaders. A former Aberdeen police chief used the working title *When Madams Reigned* for his autobiography and to describe the early years of the city. Consequently, Aberdeen was blacklisted during World War II for servicemen: You could go there, but you'd be arrested by military police if you were seen in uniform in the city limits.

Most of the city's brothels were closed by the time Kurt Cobain was born in 1967. Still, Aberdeen's reputation as a town full of "sin" made it a perfect

KURT'S TOP 50 ALBUMS

In the published version of Kurt Cobain's *Journals*, much is written about his favorite bands and albums. Cobain's "Top 50 Albums" list is the most famous example and best represents where Cobain's eclectic and earnest tastes found their center. It is noticeably lacking in Seattle and regional contemporaries because a separate list addressed acts like his mentors, the Melvins, as well as his appreciation for TAD, Screaming Trees, early Soundgarden, and Green River. Included throughout this book are hopefully useful descriptions by Andrew Earles of each of Cobain's Top 50 Albums. Here's hoping for the discovery of a few life-changing albums, as well as the revisiting of old flames.

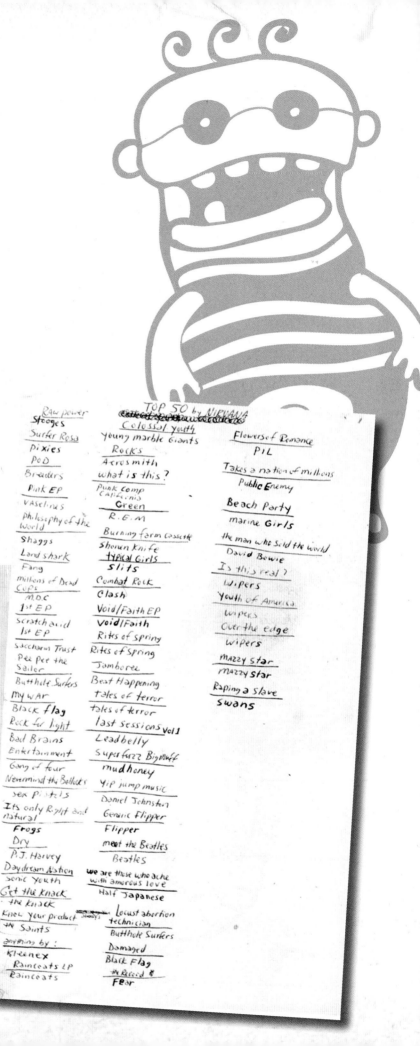

locale to birth an outsider who would rail against mainstream music norms. Cobain, in a way, was a rock outlier, much the way Nellie Cornish railed against societal sexual mores.

Most jobs in Aberdeen involved the timber industry, and during Cobain's youth his father Don worked on and off in lumberyards. Don was working as a mechanic, though, at the Chevron service station in nearby Hoquiam when Cobain was born in 1967. Don was twenty-one at the time, and his wife Wendy was only nineteen. They lived in a 300-square-foot shack that was so tiny it was behind another home and had a "half" address.

Don earned $6,000 a year as a mechanic. Logging jobs paid better, but they were also dangerous. A 1920 report from the Safety Board of Washington State called the forest products industry "more deadly than war," due to the frequent injuries caused by giant falling trees and the saws used to cut them down. Accidental amputations and death were common, as were alcoholism, domestic violence, and suicide. Unemployment was twice as high in Grays Harbor County as the rest of the state, and over-logging during the previous decades diminished even timber jobs.

Yet, for all the darkness of that backdrop, Cobain's first few years of life were not that remarkable, and his childhood was typical of a small-town upbringing. He was a popular kid in elementary and middle schools, participating in sports and afterschool activities. In his junior high yearbook photograph, he is wearing an Izod polo shirt. That year, Cobain played drums in the marching band, and his music instructor recalled him as "a regular, run-of-the-mill" student. "He was not extraordinary," the teacher remembered, "but he also wasn't awful."

Cobain was profiled in his junior high school newspaper, selected as the "Meatball of the Month." The brief article noted that his favorite song was "Don't Bring Me Down" by Electric Light Orchestra, and his favorite band was Meatloaf. Cobain would later suggest that these choices were in jest, but they were most certainly sincere at the time and reflected the same mainstream taste as his classmates. Though he later claimed his first concert was the punk rock band Black Flag, in truth the first show he attended was Sammy Hagar and Quarterflash.

He was most interested in music from decidedly middle-of-the-road rock bands (he owned all of REO Speedwagon's albums, and Beatles albums had been passed down from his aunts and uncles), but music was not yet his dominant artistic interest—drawing and painting were. It wasn't until his first used guitar at age fourteen that his interest in the guitar blossomed, but even then it involved what Cobain called "butt rock"—AC/DC, Black Sabbath, and Led Zeppelin. He began taking guitar lessons, learning "Stairway to Heaven" and "Back in Black" in the first month. He only took a few rounds of lessons, but he showed a natural talent.

Late at night, in his room by himself, he listened to Seattle radio station KISW through headphones. He heard popular hits of the day and learned to play them on his guitar with the volume turned low. There was nothing original about his playing or his interests, but it was the beginning of his craft.

KURT'S TOP 50 ALBUMS

IGGY & THE STOOGES

Raw Power (Columbia, 1973)
David Bowie rescued a label-less, post-Elektra Iggy from a lightning-fast ride down the toilet of drugs and debauchery and got him signed to Columbia and for the recording and release of the third Stooges album. Bowie was called in for an emergency, one-day mixing session on an ancient board after Iggy loaded all of the guitar on one track, vocals on a second, and the rest of the instruments on a third. The lead guitar jumps out of the classic title track like an exposed nerve and the first of two "label-required ballads" ("Gimme Danger") and remains as haunting as ever. Warts aside, *Raw Power* is still a vital inclusion in any discerning rock fan's collection. *Andrew Earles*

When Cobain was in fifth grade, his parents divorced and he later cited that singular event as the most important one in understanding his childhood—and as the moment when his angst began. Cobain was often contradictory when telling the details of his own life, and he later regretted drawing such attention to his parents' breakup. He eventually suggested that too much was made of the divorce by rock critics ("that legendary divorce was such a bore" he sang in "Serve the Servants" off *In Utero*). Still, the divorce clearly marked a shift between a Cobain described as outwardly social by his friends and family, and a child who struggled to fit in and increasingly retreated inward. He moved between his parents' homes often, and a rootlessness developed that would stay with him through the rest of his life. By losing his original nuclear family, his sense of betrayal increased. He struggled with attachment and searched for a place of belonging that no longer seemed possible in his home.

Early musical loves.

Cobain was briefly given drugs for what his family doctor diagnosed as attention deficit hyperactivity disorder, but it is no stretch to suggest that he showed signs of undiagnosed depression already. Some of that may have been due to his family life, but most was probably from genetics, or born personality.

Like any adolescent boy, his thoughts turned to sexuality, but after he had a vaguely sexual encounter with a developmentally disabled girl, his self-loathing increased, and sex and shame were forever linked. Feeling remorse over this incident, he wrote in his diary of his disgust at the girl, but he also hated himself for what he saw as himself taking advantage of her. He claimed the incident led to the local police questioning him—no police record exists, however, and no friends or family remember this detail. He wrote that he only escaped prosecution because his photo hadn't appeared in the yearbook that season, so she couldn't pick him out of it.

The story of his potential prosecution only occurred, most likely, in Cobain's head, but he did clearly have some kind of physical encounter with the girl and he felt badly about it. The incident, for all its horror, was proof, though, that Cobain was capable of compartmentalizing his own myth and exaggerating biographical details to the degree that they turned novelistic. He was becoming a storyteller, a skill that would be essential to his work as a songwriter.

The sexual shame around this brief encounter did, however, also illustrate another part of Cobain's personality that would eventually prove deadly: He wrote in his journal that he felt like jumping off a roof to his death after the incident with the girl. Depression, alcoholism, and suicide ran on both sides of his family—his maternal great-grandfather and two paternal uncles took their own lives. Cobain grew up witnessing and accepting these deaths as part of the landscape of family and of Aberdeen, where suicides were more common than in other communities. He often joked about the grisly deaths in his family and how his great-grandfather had stabbed himself in front of his children.

Just as his journal entries of his near-prosecution for a sexual crime, which read like something out of *Crime and Punishment*, alluded to suicide, his internal legend also began to involve taking his own life. At fifteen he

Butt rockin' influences.

KURT'S TOP 50 ALBUMS

PIXIES
Surfer Rosa (4AD, 1988)

The Pixies' 1988 debut full-length is one of the more crucial releases to rise from the American underground rock scene of the late 1980s. Recorded in ten days at the end of 1987, the album would go a long way in establishing Steve Albini's name as a go-to producer, his work here leading Cobain to hire him to produce *In Utero* several years later. A chaotic, catchy, and sometimes scary tour of loud/quiet and acoustic/distorted dynamics, *Surfer Rosa* opened the floodgates for the toothier works that began saturating the college-rock landscape. *AE*

made a short film that year and titled it "Kurt Commits Bloody Suicide." In the video, Cobain pretends to slice his wrists with a pop can, before dramatically falling to his death as fake blood spurts out. It was not the normal home movie of most kids his age.

Friends began to notice Cobain's differentness. "I'm going to be a superstar musician, kill myself, and go out in a flame of glory," he told one friend when he was fourteen. Cobain was under the mistaken impression at the time that Jimi Hendrix had taken his own life, and so he predicted he would die of suicide, just as Hendrix had. Teenage boys often say outrageous things without being taken seriously by their friends, and such was the case with Cobain. Still, it was just enough outside the norm that his friends recalled it vividly. Cobain was never treated for depression and never even spoke with a school counselor, as far as can be determined. Instead, he wrote out his thoughts and fears in his journals, turning his inner life into fragments of poems and, eventually, into nascent songs.

KURT'S TOP 50 ALBUMS

THE BREEDERS
The Pod (4AD, 1990)
The power struggle that was tearing the Pixies apart circa 1989's *Doolittle* all made sense when Kim Deal unleashed the debut by the Breeders, with Tanya Donelly (then of Throwing Muses, pre-Belly) on additional guitar, Josephine Wiggs on bass, and Slint drummer Britt Walford (credited as "Shannon Doughton" to maintain the illusion of a ladies-only band). Steve Albini, who helmed the Pixies' *Surfer Rosa* two years earlier, later claimed that he got the best recording and band performance of his production career on *The Pod*. In a 1992 interview with *Melody Maker*, Cobain called it one of the most influential albums of his life. *AE*

His declaration that he would find fame and then kill himself was also notable because it was one of the first times he referenced a future involving music. Prior to that, Cobain had talked about become a famous cartoonist or an animator for the Walt Disney company. Aberdeen had many nightclubs and taverns, but the only working musicians in the area were in cover bands, playing dance hits for small change. Cobain had an aunt and an uncle who played in bands, so he grew up around music and was encouraged by relatives to practice his guitar. Yet the idea of being a professional musician would have been unimaginable for most kids from Aberdeen.

In the summer of 1983, when he was sixteen, Cobain saw the local punk band the Melvins perform a concert in a grocery store parking lot. It was a show that would forever change how he thought of music and how he thought of his own musical signature. "This was what I was looking for. . . . They played faster than I ever imagined music could be played, and with more energy than my Iron Maiden records could provide," Cobain

would write in his journal. "I came to the promised land of a grocery store parking lot, and I found my special purpose."

Initially, Cobain's "purpose" was to hang around the Melvins' practice space and try to learn how to be a successful musician from a group that was anything but successful at the time. The Melvins had been named after the night manager of the local grocery store where Cobain saw them play and where their leader, Roger "Buzz" Osborne, worked. Melvins drummer Dale Crover still lived with his parents, and their house became one of the many places Cobain would hang out when he needed a meal, which became increasingly common in the next year as Cobain left home for long stretches. He would tell his father that he was with his mother, and vice versa, and instead stay with friends. Eventually, after a major dispute with his mother, not long after his sixteenth birthday, Cobain declared himself "homeless" and began sleeping on Dale Crover's porch. His parents would later suggest that it was less that they had rejected Cobain and more that he had rejected them. Kurt was a teenager, both his mother and father would attest, that they simply didn't know what to do with.

Cobain dropped out of high school that year and music became his passion, even as much of his life was focused on the struggle to find a place to live. He stayed with two informal foster families over the next year, and with friends, but was never in one place for very long. He found odd jobs where he could, with the longest stint being a summer job at the local YMCA.

In December 1985, when he was eighteen, Cobain traveled to the home of his aunt Mari in Seattle where, for the first time, he recorded some of the songs he was writing. He took Dale Crover of the Melvins with him to play drums, though Cobain played a suitcase for a drum on others. They cut nearly a dozen songs over the course of the afternoon. The tape of that session shows Cobain already skilled at crafting catchy riffs, though his frequent guitar solos, mixed at twice the volume as the other tracks, were less stellar. It was a rookie mistake—play loud, thinking it will compensate for your weaknesses. Still, considering it was Cobain's first attempt to record himself, he judged it as a success.

Local punk heroes, the Melvins, in a later 1991 photo. From left: Dale Crover, Buzz Osborne, and Lori Black. *David Corio/ Redferns/Getty Images*

A few of the songs caught on tape that day would later end up in early Nirvana set lists, but most were punk rock experiments, highlighted more by the guitar riffing than cohesive songwriting. Still, Cobain was a strong vocalist, whether screaming or singing, and his songwriting showed promise. Most of his themes were related to bodily functions or anatomy—masturbation, the female reproductive system, and defecation being frequent topics. Not surprisingly, he named this first grouping, his first band, Fecal Matter. He drew a logo that appeared as feces with steam coming off it. This was typical of Cobain's adolescent humor, but it also reflected his complete obsession with the human body in all its forms and functions. If his inner thoughts, journal entries, and sketchbooks were going to be obsessed with sperm, digestion, and grisly death, then maybe his songs would be about those topics as well.

The songs Cobain recorded that day—which are as yet unreleased, though the recordings do exist—are pedestrian compared to future Nirvana records. One tells the story of a boy who pawns his parents' wedding rings; another details how the character Buffy from the *Family Affair* television show had an unwanted pregnancy; a third is about a samurai warrior who commits suicide. But there

is a spark in the recordings, particularly in how confident Cobain sings and plays guitar.

He didn't have the songs or the licks of a real rock star, but he had the poise. He was a homeless, unemployed, high school dropout who lived on a friend's sofa in the most economically depressed town in the state, but behind that microphone, he could will himself a star. It was the one area of his life where he had self-confidence, and the one thing that would change his life.

A few years before, in high school, Cobain first met Krist Novoselic, who was two years older than Cobain. Novoselic was Croatian, one of the many immigrant nationalities that populated Aberdeen, and from a family that nearly rivaled Cobain's for dysfunction. Novoselic also fancied himself a musician, playing guitar and bass, but at the time was working at the Burger King in Aberdeen. Cobain brought a copy of the

Flyer for one of Cobain and Novoselic's earliest gigs, under the band name Skid Row at the Community World Theater in Tacoma, Washington, April 18, 1987. Aaron Burckhard was on drums.

Fecal Matter cassette to Novoselic at the fast food chain one day. Novoselic listened and heard talent, along with songs that desperately needed bass to give them punch.

The two had already jammed together on a few occasions, mostly at the Melvins' practice space, which served as a drop-in center for anyone in Grays Harbor County interested in punk rock. Novoselic's tastes were similar to Cobain's in that he enjoyed both heavy metal and punk rock. But Novoselic had a wider and a more extensive record collection, and a more even-keeled personality. Novoselic was an extrovert, gregarious and friendly, but he had enough of a sarcastic sense of humor that a true friendship was struck between the two. It would be the longest friendship Cobain would develop with another man, and the most significant.

Later both Cobain and Novoselic would attempt to shape the story of Nirvana as one of punk rock, often emphasizing that credible genre as their primary influence, particularly as Nirvana's pop success increased. Cobain once infamously accused Pearl Jam of being made up of "careerists," the suggestion being that anyone who goes into music as a career, rather than a calling, is compromised. But it says much that the first "band" that Cobain and Novoselic conceived of forming together—whether they ever played an "official" concert or not has never been clear—was to be a Creedence Clearwater Revival cover band. Given the fact that no band in Aberdeen made any money without playing covers, the idea could hardly *not* be judged "careerist." Still, the name they chose was further evidence that Cobain was playing it both ways—he wanted to call them the Sellouts. His next grouping, the second of many in that era, all formed from one party to the next, was the Stiff Woodies. They played one kegger and then dissolved.

Though Cobain very much wanted to form a serious band, and he never considered playing with anyone other than Novoselic, a sign, if nothing else, of the friendship between the two, finding a drummer was another matter. Cobain most wanted to have the Melvins' Dale Crover drum, but the Melvins had begun to get more attention and the occasional paying gig, and Crover was too serious about that band to consider a side project with little chance of success. In early 1986, Cobain and Novoselic began to play with a neighborhood drummer named Aaron Burckhard. Though they wouldn't actually use the name Nirvana for over a year, this lineup was the first incarnation of the band.

Cobain had more time, and energy, for the band than the other members. He wanted them to rehearse every day, a schedule that was hard for Burckhard and Novoselic, who both had jobs. That year Cobain moved in with Matt Lukin, who had also played in the Melvins for a time. Their little shared house—another of Cobain's many "half" addresses, again behind another larger home—became the band's rehearsal space when they didn't play in Novoselic's mother's hair salon.

Cobain was twenty years old. He met his first serious girlfriend that year, Tracy Marander, at a punk rock show he attended with the Melvins. So many of the connections in his life had sprung from the Melvins, even love.

KURT'S TOP 50 ALBUMS

THE VASELINES
Dying For It EP (53rd & 3rd, 1988)
The Glasgow wünderkinds' second EP features four songs of folk-pop (or as it would come to be known, "twee-pop") genius, including the infectious "Molly's Lips," covered to great rocking effect by Nirvana and a highlight of their *Incesticide* outtakes and B-sides collection. Following the Vaselines' demise, Eugene Kelly went on to form the more rocking Eugenius in the early 1990s. *AE*

In early March 1987, the band had their first public performance. The location was less than glamorous: an unpaid gig at a kegger in nearby Raymond. Cobain hadn't yet settled on a name, but was considering Poo Poo Box or Gut Bomb, among others. The gig did not go particularly well. The drunken kids in attendance urged the band to play Led Zeppelin. Cobain eventually acceded and performed "Heartbreaker." A fight ensued between Novoselic's girlfriend and another partygoer. Cobain felt he had problems with the crude PA, an occurrence that would haunt him for his entire performing career.

But the gig went well enough, or at least was satisfactory enough to Cobain, that more were set up. Over the course of the next year, music went from a hobby for Cobain to an obsession that dominated every aspect of his life. For a kid who had struggled to fit in since the onset of adolescence, being a bandleader gave him an identity he had been searching for his whole life.

Two months after the Raymond kegger, Cobain moved to Olympia to live with his girlfriend Tracy. In many ways it was an ideal shift for Cobain. His girlfriend was hardworking and industrious, and she supported him when he couldn't find work, which

Flyer, Community World Theater, Tacoma, Washington, June 27, 1987. Cobain, Novoselic, and Burckhard performed as Pen Cap Chew.

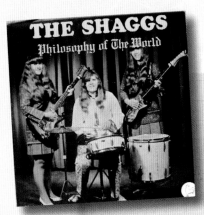

KURT'S TOP 50 ALBUMS

THE SHAGGS
Philosophy of the World
(Third World Records, 1969)
The sole album by the Wiggins sisters (Dot, Betty, Helen, and Rachel) is a one of the first celebrated albums of the type later known as "outsider" music. *Philosophy of the World* is front-to-back naïve, endearing ineptitude that would impact an entire generation of DIY just-pick-it-up-and-play bands, most notably Beat Happening, as well as the more acoustic tendencies of the riot grrrl movement. The long-defunct band (originally the brainchild of the Wiggins sisters' father, Austin) garnered some posthumous acclaim with a 1980 reissue (after the band NRBQ discovered it buried in a radio station record library in 1978), which only grew with time. *AE*

was often. He did briefly find employment at a motel, and later as a janitor, but thoughts of his band were so overpowering that he barely had the space to think of anything else. Novoselic was living in Tacoma, and Burckhard was still in Aberdeen, so rehearsals meant hours of driving. Yet Cobain insisted they practice many times a week. They got better quickly, but real success was slow to come.

The gigs that followed included opening slots at the Community World Theater, a former adult movie hall in Tacoma. At most of those shows, the audiences were made up of a few dozen punk rock fans, and bands were rarely paid more than gas money. The band's name was still fluid—they would perform as Bliss, Pen Cap Chew, and a few other names before Cobain finally settled on Nirvana after several dozen shows. The drummer position shifted a few times and the band was using Dave Foster when the band played their first-ever Seattle concert. There were only a few dozen in attendance at the tiny club called the Vogue, but when Cobain played "Love Buzz," the only cover in the band's set but also the song that seemed the biggest crowd pleaser, his guitar prowess drew attention. Cobain would play the song's solo lying on the stage floor, moving around in a circle. It was one of his only stage tricks, but it was effective, and after the gig, the band's notice rose in Seattle. It says much about what a different world Aberdeen was from Seattle, that Cobain was so afraid to be in the big city that he feared he would be held up before the gig. For all his punk rock posturing, he was a small-town boy at heart.

The band also ventured to Seattle on January 23, 1988, for their first recording session as a band,

and Cobain's first attempt since his crude teenaged recordings at his aunt's house. Spying an ad in Seattle magazine *The Rocket* for a studio that charged only $20 an hour, Cobain booked time at Reciprocal with producer Jack Endino. Endino had begun to record a few of the rising Seattle bands of the era for Sub Pop Records, but Cobain didn't know that at the time, and was drawn only by the cheap rates. Endino knew so little about the band, or Cobain, that he wrote down Cobain's name as "Kurt Covain" when he logged the session into the schedule. Cobain and Novoselic convinced Dale Crover to play with them, and so the three of them drove up to Seattle in a friend's pickup that had a shingle-covered camper on the back and contained a working woodstove. It was a scene straight out of *The Beverly Hillbillies*, this little smoke-spewing camper parked in front of a Seattle recording studio.

KURT'S TOP 50 ALBUMS

FANG

Landshark (Boner Records, 1983)
Ahead-of-the-curve metallic punk rock from San Francisco's East Bay with a nasty sense of humor and a nastier sense of melody, Fang, and it's debut album, has never received its due because of singer Sam "Sammytown" McBride's drug-fueled murder of his girlfriend in 1989 and subsequent six-year prison stretch. Guitarist Tom Flynn first formed the Boner label to release early Fang records, but grew a roster that would include classic records by the Melvins, Steel Pole Bath Tub, MDC, Superconductor (first band of New Pornographer Carl Newman), and Verbal Abuse. Both Nirvana and Mudhoney covered Landshark opener "The Money Will Roll Right In." *AE*

Flyer, Community World Theater, Tacoma, Washington, August 9, 1987. Cobain, Novoselic, and Burckhard performed as Bliss.

They played for several hours and Cobain paid the $152 bill with cash. They managed to record ten songs, some of which they had played at their very first Raymond concert, but a few others that Cobain had written that month. Most were punk rock noise experiments, but on songs like "Floyd the Barber" and "Downer," Cobain was already displaying a penchant for writing crunchy guitar riffs. They had to leave the studio quickly to make a show they had scheduled in Tacoma, so they worked efficiently and impressed Endino.

The revolving drum stool continued to be a problem, as Crover was often not available due to Melvins commitments. Cobain placed several ads in *The Rocket* seeking a permanent drummer. Then at a show at the Community World Theater in early 1988, Cobain and Novoselic met Chad Channing and took notice of his huge North drum kit, by far the largest kit on the stage that night, and played by a drummer of almost elfin-proportions, as Channing was only 5 foot 6 inches, even shorter than Cobain. Typical of Cobain's general indirect communication style, he never asked Channing to join the band, but instead kept calling and asking Channing to rehearsals until Channing became their de facto drummer. Channing stayed with the band longer than any drummer other than Dave Grohl.

With gigs, a new drummer, a benefactor in his girlfriend, and a few dozen punkers who called themselves fans, Cobain set himself toward breaking his band to the next level. That meant putting out an album or a single, so he began to send demo cassettes to independent labels he hoped to snare into releasing their music. It was an era when major record labels dominated the industry, but there were dozens of smaller independent labels like SST and Touch and Go that released up-and-coming bands. There wasn't much money to be made in that world without touring extensively, but it was the best place to start, and Cobain promoted his band fiercely, writing hundreds of letters to indie labels.

It is impossible to determine exactly how many of these letters Cobain sent out, but many drafts exist in his journals. He wrote to every label he could think of in an effort he sustained for many months.

He didn't get a single reply.

KURT'S TOP 50 ALBUMS

MDC

Millions of Dead Cops (R Radical, 1982)
This Austin, Texas, band was known as the Stains before relocating to San Francisco and undergoing a name-change to MDC (hint: this is a self-titled album). MDC released this militantly political thrust of thoroughly fierce buzzsaw hardcore on their own label and toured the country in highly confrontational style, courtesy of founder Dave Dictor (later a columnist for hardcore bible *Maximumrocknroll*), a former hippie who found hardcore's ideals amenable and enjoyed testing their boundaries and the beliefs of his brethren. *AE*

Kurt Cobain's 1960s Mosrite Gospel Guitar. This was one of two actual Mosrites he owned. Cobain painted the small Mosrite dot markers with white-out to make them more visible in a dark, concert setting. This is a factory right-handed instrument, so Cobain modified it with a strap button added to the treble side horn and flipped the original metal string guide to allow it to be strung left-handed. *Heritage Auctions*

Cobain and Novoselic's first band was built on the dream of being a Creedence Clearwater Revival cover band.

Opposite: Nirvana photographed in Seattle in May 1988. From left, drummer Chad Channing, Novoselic, and Cobain. *Charles Peterson/Retna Ltd./Corbis*

KURT'S TOP 50 ALBUMS

SCRATCH ACID
Scratch Acid EP (Rabid Cat, 1984)

The awesomely named Scratch Acid (whatever it means) took the sound of fellow Texans the Butthole Surfers, wound it tightly with a thick, abrasive affinity for Nick Cave's Birthday Party, and birthed an early version of what would be called "noise rock" as the 1980s came to a close. However, the band is possibly more famous for providing a pre–Jesus Lizard outlet for vocalist David Yow and guitarist David Wm. Sims, before the latter joined Steve Albini for his pre-Shellac venture, Rapeman. Drummer Rey Washam is the Carmen Appice of American hardcore, post-hardcore, and related styles, having hit the skins for Ministry, Big Boys, TAD, Lard, Helios Creed, the Didjits, and the aforementioned Rapeman. *AE*

In 1988, things did begin to look up for the band slightly. Their live shows were drawing slightly larger audiences, and though they were still crowds that could be counted in the dozens, they were consistent. Nirvana expanded their turf to include Olympia and the occasional show in Seattle. Jack Endino had been sufficiently impressed with their demo tape that he gave a copy to a DJ at KCMU, the University of Washington's college radio station, and one of the tracks began to get airplay.

Endino also gave a copy of the demo to Jonathan Poneman, who, with his partner Bruce Pavitt, had started Sub Pop Records. The Seattle music scene was still dominated by cover bands, but Sub Pop had begun to have minor success with alternative bands, and a few clubs were booking original bands. Though Sub Pop was still a shoestring effort, Cobain had not written them the same plea he'd mailed to every other indie label in the nation. But they were on the rise and getting positive notices in the press for their few releases to date. Poneman and Pavitt liked the Nirvana recording and a meeting was set up at a coffee shop in Seattle's Capitol Hill neighborhood.

KURT'S TOP 50 ALBUMS

SACCHARINE TRUST
Paganicons EP (SST, 1981)

The emergence and growth of traditional hardcore, namely in ground-zero late-1970s/early-1980s Los Angeles, tends to overshadow the individualistic leftfield undercurrents that bubbled up in the same region. Saccharine Trust wielded free-jazz, U.K. post-punk, and beat poetry influences as often as they did hardcore tempos on this debut EP and its subsequent 1984 full-length, *Surviving You Always*, also on SST. Guitarist Joe Biaza, a frequent Minutemen, Greg Ginn, Mike Watt (solo), and Nels Cline collaborator, provides the band's extra-special touch. *AE*

The meeting, according to all, was just short of a disaster. Novoselic usually acted as manager, handling business arrangements (he was the only member who had graduated from high school), but he showed up swilling from a bottle of wine. Cobain was extremely nervous and withdrawn. Poneman offered them a recording deal, but only to put out a single and only to pay for recording costs. Worse, Poneman was interested only in "Love Buzz," the one song in Nirvana's set Cobain didn't write. Yet, at the end of the meeting, Nirvana accepted the agreement, which was finalized by handshake, and the band scheduled time to record with Endino again.

Cobain was ready for things to move quickly, but in the band's early days things were never speedy enough for him. Endino didn't have an opening until the second week of June, and that wasn't solid. Sub Pop's financial situation was so precarious that Cobain received a phone call from Pavitt asking if Cobain could front $200 for the costs. Eventually, the label scraped up the money elsewhere and Nirvana headed into the studio on June 11 to cut their first single.

Opposite: An early portrait of Nirvana in Seattle in May 1988 by noted scene photographer Charles Peterson. Top to bottom: Krist Novoselic, Chad Channing, and Kurt Cobain. *Charles Peterson/Retna Ltd./Corbis. Below:* Nirvana's first single, "Love Buzz"/"Big Cheese," featuring Alice Wheeler photos. The single was released in autumn 1987 as part of Sub Pop's Singles Club.

This session did not go as smoothly as their previous one. It took them five hours to finish one song. They returned for two other sessions in the month that followed, spending a total of thirteen hours during this first studio span that produced only four tracks: "Love Buzz," "Big Cheese," and two others.

The release was further delayed when Sub Pop announced that they planned to release the record as part of their Singles Club, a subscription-type service with only a few copies available for sale in stores. Cobain wanted to balk at this, but as he had no written contract with the label, and no other prospects, he agreed.

The "Love Buzz" single finally came out that fall. The initial press run was only a thousand copies, of which the band was given several dozen. Cobain drove to KCMU to drop off a copy, hoping it would soar to the top of the station's charts. KCMU—which decades later would turn into powerhouse KEXP—was then operating with such a weak signal it could only be picked up within a few miles of the university campus. Cobain was living in Olympia at the time, where he couldn't get the station's signal, so after dropping the record off at the station he stayed parked in his car for hours, hoping to hear the station play it. They did not. Frustrated, he finally called the station, disguising his voice and requesting his own song.

Thirty minutes later the station played "Love Buzz", and for the first time in his life, Cobain heard himself on the radio. He was essentially penniless, living off his girlfriend, and leading a band with only a few dozen fans. He was still a year away from recording *Bleach*, Nirvana's debut album, and three years away from *Nevermind*, the album that would change the entire music world. But on that day, for a kid born and raised in Aberdeen, hearing the sound of his voice on the radio was the stuff of dreams.

He had willed himself to become a musician, to create a band, to write songs, to make a record, and now to get that record played on the radio, even if it was played only because he spent a quarter in a payphone to request it. But to Kurt Cobain, that moment was magic.

2. IN BLOOM
THE *BLEACH* YEARS

By Gillian G. Gaar

January 23, 1988, would prove to be the most important date in Nirvana's history. It was on this day that events were set in motion that would place the band on the path to worldwide acclaim.

No one suspected this at the time, of course. As the year began, Kurt Cobain and Krist Novoselic weren't even in a proper band. After an August 9, 1987, performance at the Community World Theater in Tacoma, the band had fallen apart. But before too long, Cobain, who'd moved to Olympia to live with his girlfriend Tracy Marander, contacted Novoselic, who'd moved to Tacoma with his girlfriend, Shelli Dilly, about reviving the group. They didn't bother contacting their previous drummer, Aaron Burckhard; Cobain felt he lacked sufficient dedication. Instead, he placed an ad in the October 1987 issue of Seattle's monthly music paper *The Rocket*: "SERIOUS DRUMMER WANTED. Underground attitude, Black Flag, Melvins, Zeppelin, Scratch Acid, Ethel Merman. Versatile as heck." The ad failed to produce any results, so Cobain and Novoselic practiced with Melvins drummer Dale Crover until they could find a permanent drummer.

But Cobain was eager to take the next step and couldn't wait to hear how his songs sounded when recorded in a professional studio. Through *The Rocket* and album credits on locally released records, he'd learned about Reciprocal Recording, a Seattle studio that was both cheap and where albums he'd liked, such as Soundgarden's *Screaming Life*, were recorded. When he phoned the studio to book a session, in-house producer

Above: Seattle colleagues. *Opposite:* Kurt Cobain plays his guitar in Seattle on September 22, 1990. *Ian Tilton/Corbis*

29

Left: Flyer, Community World Theater, Tacoma, Washington, March 19, 1988. This show heralded the first time Cobain and Novoselic played under the name Nirvana. Dave Foster was on drums. Right: Flyer, Lame Fest, Moore Theatre, Seattle, Washington, June 9, 1988.

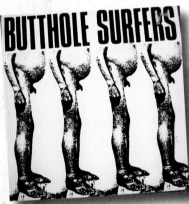

KURT'S TOP 50 ALBUMS

BUTTHOLE SURFERS

The Butthole Surfers EP (a.k.a. *Pee Pee the Sailor* and *Brown Reason to Live*) (Alternative Tentacles, 1983) Usually known as *Brown Reason to Live*, the 1983 debut recording by the Butthole Surfers was, like Flipper's *Generic* and the Void side of *Faith/Void*, one of the great (and successful) attempts to deregulate American hardcore punk. Employing early rumblings of the Texas band's later interpretation of "psychedelia" (plodding drums, distorted and heavy bass, absurdist toilet-talk lyrics), the EP is a true original with no sonic or aesthetic warning shot in the history of underground rock. *AE*

Jack Endino took the call. A guitarist in the band Skin Yard, Endino had become the go-to producer for the label that had released *Screaming Life*, as well as records by Seattle bands Green River and Mudhoney: Sub Pop.

Mishearing Cobain's name over the telephone, Endino scheduled the January 23 session for "Kurt Covain." The musicians arrived at Reciprocal around noon and went straight to work, recording ten songs in four hours. There was minimal overdubbing; after laying down the backing tracks, Cobain recorded his vocals in one take (Crover also added backing vocals to "Downer" and "Spank Thru"). "I just started at the top of the reel and pressed 'record,' he'd sing it and then go, 'Okay, next!'" Endino recalled. "And I'd go, 'Okay,' and press 'record' again."

Most of the songs Nirvana chose to record were fixtures in the band's set list. "Spank Thru" and "Downer" dated back to Cobain's Fecal Matter days. Both songs, as well as "Hairspray Queen," "Mexican Seafood," "Pen Cap Chew," and "Floyd the Barber," had been performed in the band's live radio appearance

Above: University of Washington HUB Ballroom. *Charles Peterson/Retna Ltd./Corbis.* Left: Nirvana recorded Kiss' "Do You Love Me" from *Destroyer* for the August 1990 Kiss tribute album, *Hard to Believe.*

on Evergreen State College station KAOS the previous May. All their practicing since then had paid off; the band sounded far more confident, and Crover's drumming gave the songs more power. Some numbers were still derivative. "Beeswax" rambled to no clear effect, "Paper Cuts" was an obvious Melvins knock-off, and "Aero Zeppelin" revealed its influences in its very title. But "Floyd The Barber" (in which the small-town residents of the TV program *The Andy Griffith Show* are transformed into something out of David Lynch's surreal *Twin Peaks*) stands out as an original, a vivid reflection of Cobain's own twisted worldview, and made all the more forceful by Crover's drumming.

Recording was finished around 4 p.m., and mixing was finished two hours later; the band then had to leave for a show at the Community World Theater. Endino asked if he could hold on to the eight-track master so he could make a copy of the session for himself. Saying "yes" was the best decision the band ever made,

Left: Flyer, Hal Holmes Community Center, Ellensburg, Washington, June 17, 1988.
Right: Flyer, Sub Pop Sunday at the Vogue, Seattle, Washington, July 3, 1988.

KURT'S TOP 50 ALBUMS

BLACK FLAG
My War (SST, 1984)

In 1984 alone, Black Flag played 178 shows around the world and released (the double-length) *Live '84* and *three* studio albums. Just reading that sentence would make most bands tired. While the six songs on side one of *My War* are of hardcore tempo and feel like an extension of the classic *Damaged*, the three tracks (each over six minutes long) on side two find Black Flag exploring the slowest, heaviest riffs and rhythms this side of early-1970s Black Sabbath or the underground doom metal bands of the day like Trouble, Pentagram, Witchmaster General, and soon-to-be label-mates Saint Vitus. As such, *My War* informed the Melvins' mid-period slowdown, Nirvana's *Bleach*, and the sludge/stoner-metal movement that grew to prominence in the early 1990s. *AE*

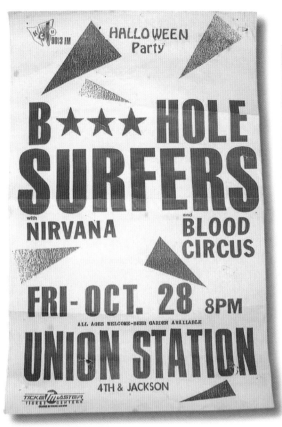

Left: Flyer, Union Station, Seattle, Washington, October 28, 1988. *Middle:* Flyer, Speedy O'Tubbs Rhythmic Underground, Bellingham, Washington, November 23, 1988. *Artist: Jim Blanchard Right:* Flyer, East Ballroom, Husky Union Building, University of Washington, Seattle, Washington, February 25, 1989.

for Endino passed on a copy of the tape (known as the "Dale Demo" because of Crover's participation) to Jonathan Poneman, Sub Pop's cofounder. The label was always on the lookout for new acts, and Poneman listened to the tape with interest. He was immediately taken by the opening number, "If You Must," which begins with Cobain singing quietly, then lets loose with an almighty roar; Cobain's voice would always be the most distinctive element of Nirvana's music. Poneman wasted no time contacting Cobain.

Cobain hadn't been thinking of approaching Sub Pop. He'd sent off copies of the demo to labels with a higher profile: Alternative Tentacles (home of Dead Kennedys), SST (Black Flag, Meat Puppets, Hüsker Dü), and Touch and Go (Scratch Acid, Big Black). But he was open to Sub Pop's pitch, and Poneman arranged for the band to play a few Seattle shows so his partner, Bruce Pavitt, could see them in action.

Of more immediate concern was the need for a new drummer. The Melvins were relocating to California; when another ad in *The Rocket* ("DRUMMER WANTED. Play hard, sometimes light, underground, versatile, fast, medium, slow, versatile, serious, heavy, versatile, dorky, nirvana, hungry") failed to generate any candidates, Crover recommended Aberdeen drummer Dave Foster. One of Foster's early shows with the band, on March 19, 1988, at the Community World Theater, also unveiled a new name for the group: Nirvana. Cobain later offered various explanations for the name, with his simple comment to *Submerge*—"There's no reason at all, it just sounded nice"—probably the most accurate.

But Foster's tenure was short-lived. Cobain was almost immediately unhappy with his new drummer and, unknown to Foster, placed another ad that ran in *The Rocket* in May even as Foster was still playing with the group ("DRUMMER WANTED. Hard, heavy, to

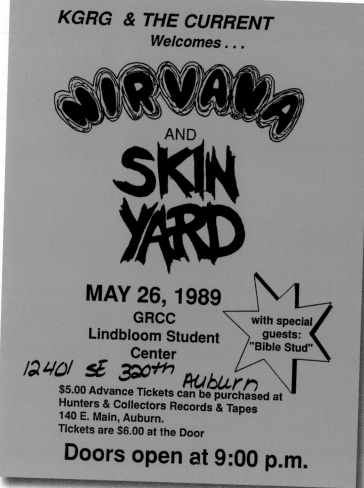

Left: Flyer, Reko/Muse, Olympia, Washington, April Fools' Day, 1989. *Right:* Flyer, Lindbloom Student Center, Green River Community College, Auburn, Washington, May, 26, 1989. *Opposite:* Cobain and Everman, 1989. *Charles Peterson*

KURT'S TOP 50 ALBUMS

BAD BRAINS

Rock for Light (PVC, 1983)

In the nascent days of hardcore punk, the fastest, tightest, most complex, and intense act in the land comprised four dudes who began as a jazz-fusion band called Mind Power but became devout African-American Rastafarians on the road to punk rock obsession. Bad Brains' self-titled 1982 debut is built with the band's unparalleled fast-core next to genuine endeavors in reggae. On Bad Brains' second album, *Rock for the Light*, not only does the trick work, but it *kills*. Produced by the Cars' Ric Ocasek, *Rock for Light* features six rerecorded tracks from the 1982 debut. *AE*

hell with your 'looks and hair a must.' Soundgarden, Zep, Scratch Acid"). To Cobain, Foster represented the isolated, backwoods world of Aberdeen that Cobain was desperate to leave behind. When Foster was arrested for fighting, losing his driver's license as a result, Cobain began to ease him out of the band, telling him Nirvana was on hiatus. Cobain and Novoselic briefly rehearsed with Aaron Burckhard again, though Burckhard also fell afoul of the law, arrested for drunk driving in Cobain's car.

With Sub Pop offering Nirvana the chance to record a single, Cobain and Novoselic approached another drummer they'd seen playing at local shows: Chad Channing. Channing was born in 1967 in Santa Rosa, California, and had taught himself to play guitar,

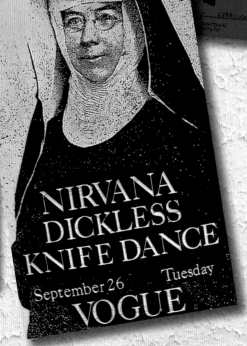

Top: Flyer, Covered Wagon Saloon, San Francisco, California, June 22, 1989. *Left:* Flyer, the Sonic Temple, Masonic Temple, Wilkinsburg, Pennsylvania, July 9, 1989. *Middle:* Flyer, the Vogue, Seattle, Washington, September 29, 1989. *Right:* Flyer, Rockin' T.P., Santa Fe, New Mexico, June 27, 1989. *Artist: Brian Curley*

One of Chad Channing's drumsticks from a Los Angeles gig on the *Bleach* tour. *Kevin Estrada*

KURT'S TOP 50 ALBUMS

GANG OF FOUR

Entertainment! (EMI/Warner Bros., 1979)
The cream of the U.K. post-punk crop (mostly a British phenomenon to begin with), *Entertainment!* is a forward-thinking rearrangement of punk rock filtered through funk, disco, jazz-fusion (specifically Ornette Coleman's Prime Time Band of the late-1970s), dub, and traditional reggae. As with contemporaries the Pop Group and, in the States, Pere Ubu, Gang of Four put the bass front and center, giving most of the songs a very danceable beat that thumps through the clean if not scratchy guitar attack and shouted, sung, or spoken lyrics high in sociopolitical content. *Entertainment!* was also a huge influence on acts as disparate as R.E.M., Fugazi, and the Red Hot Chili Peppers. *AE*

bass, and drums in his teens while recovering from an accident. At the time he met Cobain and Novoselic, Channing was playing drums in the Magnet Men (later Tic-Dolly-Row) with future Soundgarden bassist Ben Shepherd.

Following a show at the Community World Theater on May 21, Cobain and Novoselic asked Channing if he'd be interested in joining Nirvana. A surprised Channing demurred, though he agreed to practice with them. One practice led to another, and when he was asked to play a show with the band, Channing agreed, though he never formally stated he would join Nirvana. It was typical of the band's passive-aggressive nature. Similarly, Foster was never told he was out of the band; he learned he'd been replaced when he saw an ad for an upcoming Nirvana show in *The Rocket*.

At last Nirvana had a stable lineup, one that would stay together for the next two years, giving the band a solid base from which to grow. A recording session for the band's first single was set up at Reciprocal on June 11. Pavitt and Poneman had suggested recording "Love Buzz"; Cobain wasn't happy about having to record a cover instead of an original number, but acquiesced.

It was actually an astute song choice; though a pop song, Nirvana's version lashed the number to a fuzzy, hypnotic groove, differentiating it substantially from the original version by Dutch band Shocking Blue. The droning "Blandest" was initially planned as the B-side, but no one felt it really gelled in the studio (it was

later released on the *With the Lights Out* box set), so "Big Cheese" was chosen, its sarcastic lyrics inspired by what Cobain felt was the Poneman's judgmental posturing. The band also recorded early versions of "Sifting," "Mr. Moustache," and "Blew" at the session. At a second session on June 30, the band rerecorded "Floyd the Barber," but it lacked the forcefulness of Dave Crover's version and was recorded over. A new version of "Spank Thru" was rerecorded as well, in a higher key than the Dale Demo version. At a third session on July 16, Cobain rerecorded a new vocal for "Love Buzz."

Slowly but surely, Nirvana's profile was continuing to rise locally. In July, they played their first show opening for an out-of-town act, Los Angeles band the Leaving Trains (in an eerie footnote, the show's co-promoter, Nikolas Hartshorne, was the medical examiner who would perform Cobain's autopsy). In October they opened for the Butthole Surfers, and in December they opened for Canadian punk act D.O.A. The first-ever article on the band also appeared in the August/September 1988 issue of *Backlash*, a music paper edited by Dawn Anderson, Endino's girlfriend at the time. The article, by Anderson, entitled "It May Be the Devil and It May Be the Lord But It Sure as Hell Ain't Human," has been subsequently quoted in virtually every Nirvana biography for its bold

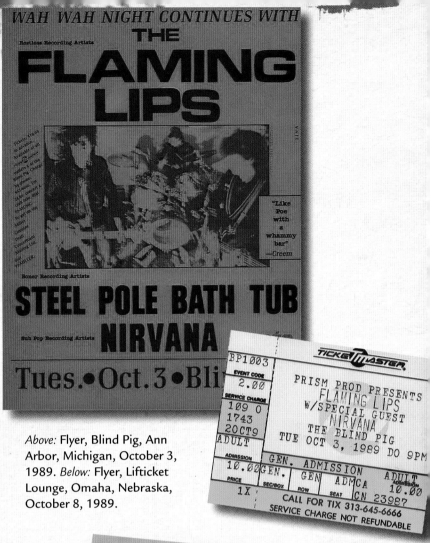

Above: Flyer, Blind Pig, Ann Arbor, Michigan, October 3, 1989. *Below:* Flyer, Lifticket Lounge, Omaha, Nebraska, October 8, 1989.

Opposite: Novoselic and Cobain with Mudhoney's Dan Peters, who took over Nirvana's drum stool during downtime from his regular band. In the excellent Mudhoney documentary *I'm Now*, Peters recalls Dave Grohl hanging out at this photo shoot; unbeknownst to Peters, the decision had already been made to replace him. *Ian Tilton/S.I.N./Alamy*

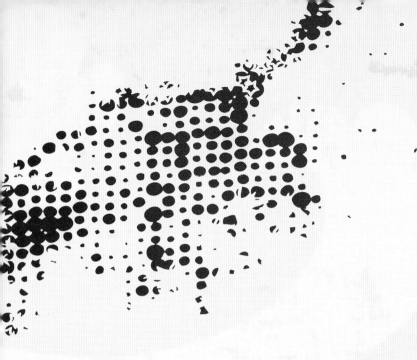

KURT'S TOP 50 ALBUMS

SEX PISTOLS

Never Mind the Bollocks, Here's the Sex Pistols (Virgin/Warner Bros., 1977)
Built from four previously released U.K. singles and filled out with perpetually troubled and stunted studio work in late 1976 and early 1977, the Sex Pistols' only proper studio album is the one punk rock record from which even the most strident anti-punk music fan has heard at least one track ("Anarchy in the U.K."). Released by Virgin after the band was dropped by their original label, A&M, the album benefited from heightened exposure (it went to No. 1 in the U.K.), due to the band's notorious nature, and most likely can be credited with introducing the world to punk. *AE*

prediction: "At the risk of sounding blasphemous, I honestly believe that with enough practice, Nirvana could become—*better than the Melvins!*"

Anderson's article also plugged the upcoming single, but its release was delayed until November, due to Sub Pop's perennial cash flow problems. When it finally appeared, it received a good reception; because of the song's obscurity, many people weren't even aware that "Love Buzz" was a cover. The following month saw the release of *Sub Pop 200*, a three-EP box set that featured the June 30, 1988, recording of "Spank Thru" (featuring a backing vocal from Endino). This set caught the attention of BBC Radio 1 DJ John Peel, who favorably reviewed it in British newspaper *The Observer*. It was good news for Sub Pop, as well as the other acts that appeared on the set.

Best of all for the band, Nirvana was heading back into the studio to record their first album. Though Sub Pop was only interested in an EP, the band wanted to release a full-length album and decided to go ahead and pay the recording costs themselves; a friend of Channing's, guitarist Jason Everman, agreed to put up the money for the sessions: $606.17, as famously noted on the album's sleeve. The LP was recorded and mixed at Reciprocal over the course of six sessions: December 24 and December 29 to 31, 1988, and January 14 and 24, 1989.

As Cobain later told *Sounds*, "Most of the lyrics on the *Bleach* album are about life in Aberdeen." And certainly the characters depicted in the new songs were ones he knew well. "Mr. Moustache" is a caricature of a redneck macho man, the title partially inspired by the flak some of Nirvana's drummers received for having moustaches (moustaches weren't very punk rock). "Swap Meet" revisited the flea market setting of the earlier song "Mrs. Butterworth," focusing on a couple that ekes out a living selling crafts on the flea market circuit. In "Negative Creep," the narrator revels in his own unpleasantness.

Above: Flyer, Riverside, Newcastle upon Tyne, Great Britain, October 23, 1989. *Right:* 1989 Nirvana T-shirt. *www.WycoVintage.com. Below:* Flyer, Edward's No. 8, Birmingham, Great Britain, October 29, 1989.

Other songs took shots at standard targets: "Sifting" attacks authority figures, while "School" distills the bitterness of being excluded from a social scene to a taut fifteen-word rant. "School" was meant as a stinging riposte to the insularity of the Seattle music scene; similarly, "Blew" and "About a Girl" presented an equally pessimistic view of personal relationships. The very first line of "Blew" alludes to being suffocated, and, despite its pretty melody, the lyrics of "About a Girl" have an underlying resentfulness, particularly in the chorus, when the narrator sings about taking advantage of his partner, who herself has no qualms about hanging him out to dry. It was a typical sentiment; Cobain would never write a straightforward love song.

But in other ways, "About a Girl" was Cobain's—and Nirvana's—first step into a larger world. Melodically, the song was unadulterated pop; Cobain said he'd

THE ALBUMS

BLEACH

by Andrew Earles

Famously recorded at Jack Endino's Reciprocal Studios for $606.17, Nirvana's debut album, *Bleach*, released on June 15, 1989, is the sound of a band finding its footing. As Kurt Cobain apologetically stressed in post-*Nevermind* interviews, it is also the sound of a band adhering to the "Sub Pop sound" (i.e., an early version of what would soon become known the world over as "grunge"). While notable, such claims are questionable in hindsight.

Though Cobain allegedly told Soundgarden's Kim Thayil that the latter's band was Nirvana's biggest influence at the time of *Bleach*, the album does not reflect early Soundgarden. The album is a much catchier translation of Cobain's early mentors, the Melvins, but it is an interpretation nonetheless, which further distances *Bleach*, for those paying attention or with savvy enough ears, from the standard-issue grunge that Cobain and the critics have classified it as. The metallic sound is a dominating sonic trademark of the album, but it must be noted that this sound is influenced by the underground metal environment of the 1980s (i.e., punked-up Black Sabbath riffing plus the influence of 1980s thrash metal that informed American hardcore before, during, and after *Bleach* was recorded), not the mainstream Sunset Strip metal that was, and still is, most widely associated with the term "metal."

Recorded in December 1988 and January 1989, *Bleach* is an excellent example of the abrasive, somewhat sloppy but pop-driven indie-rock albums from the genre's early days, and would sonically fit into the sub-genre of Midwestern noise-rock that labels like Amphetamine Reptile in Minneapolis and Touch and Go in Chicago were releasing in the mid- to late 1980s. In fact, Nirvana was not under contract to Sub Pop when the recordings were made. The soon-to-be Pacific Northwest power/safe-house had released "Love Buzz," a Shocking Blue cover and Nirvana's recorded debut (which launched Sub Pop's infamous Singles Club in November 1988), but had only expressed interest in releasing a follow-up EP. Given Sub Pop's noncommittal stance on a new Nirvana LP and the facts that they were not yet an established entity and already had a reputation for terrifying insolvency, Cobain wanted to shop the finished recordings to Touch and Go and SST. But after bassist Krist Novoselic drunkenly showed up on Sub Pop cofounder Bruce Pavitt's front step shortly after the recordings were finished and demanded that Nirvana be contracted to release *Bleach*, the band became the first that the label ever honored with such a formal arrangement. Fortuitously, said arrangement would fund Sub Pop throughout the early 1990s—*Nevermind*'s mega-success not only created great demand for its predecessor, but Sub Pop was able to use the *Bleach* contract as leverage with *Nevermind* label Geffen to negotiate a small percentage of the second album's sales.

The most powerful tracks on *Bleach* are undoubtedly "School," "Negative Creep," "Paper Cuts," and "Swap Meet". (One could also include "Downer," one of two bonus tracks on Sub Pop's 1992 reissue.) All fall into the indie noise-rock template, but are sterling examples thereof. Opener "Blew" reveals a clearly confident Cobain on guitar and is bolstered by a lead rather than a riff—one that the guitarist sings with the chorus in a nod to TAD, who were close friends and another mentoring force. But the song that had everyone discussing widespread "potential" was the album's lone, unabashed pop number, "About a Girl." The track sticks out of the sometimes antagonistic, riff-saturated set like a fuzzy artifact from one of Nirvana's East Coast indie contemporaries (perhaps a band from the Homestead roster). Cobain was hesitant to include the song, voicing his concern to producer Endino, but in the end a "who cares?" verdict won out. Almost all biographical texts about the band state that the lyrics for "About a Girl" were scrawled across scratch paper on the dashboard of the band's tour van as they motored through rural Washington, an early logistical inconvenience necessary to get all three band members to one destination.

Though he is credited in the liner notes (and footed the recording tab), Jason Everman only filled the second guitar slot for part of Nirvana's national tour (the band's first) in support of the *Bleach*. Also notable is the fact there are two drummers on *Bleach*, and neither one is named Dave Grohl. Nirvana's first official drummer, Chad Channing, can be heard on nine of the original vinyl release's eleven tracks. The remaining two—"Floyd the Barber" and "Paper Cuts" (and also bonus track "Downer")—were recorded during an earlier January 1988 demo session with Melvins drummer Dale Crover handling the kit. The tracks were rerecorded during the *Bleach* sessions, but Crover's versions were preferred for the final set.

Instrumentally, Nirvana was rehearsed and efficient in the studio, although Cobain did take the time to labor over his lyrics. "School" details the high school–like nature of the Seattle music scene, "Floyd the Barber" is a twisted riff on characters from *The Andy Griffith Show*, and "Swap Meet" is based on a man and woman get by selling bric-a-brac at a flea market. "Negative Creep" and "Scoff" are typical paeans to the self-worthlessness that "Kurdt Kobain" (as he credited himself on the album's back sleeve) would never totally outgrow.

Bleach would sell 1.7 million copies by 2003, and it remains the bestselling album in Sub Pop's long and storied catalog. Before the release of *Nevermind*, Sub Pop moved 40,000 copies of *Bleach*, in all of its scruffy glory, in just less than two years—very respectable numbers for a pre-Internet indie release that speak to the merits of the label, the band, and the album. *Bleach* wasn't just a good record that happened to be followed by a great record from a greatly improved band.

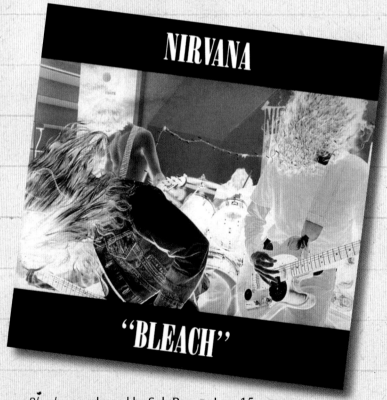

Bleach was released by Sub Pop on June 15, 1989, although early copies were sold at the label's Lame Fest on June 9.

Left: Nirvana plays live at the School of Oriental and African Studies, London, promoting *Bleach. Ed Sirrs/ Camera Press*.
Below: Flyer, Student Union, School of Oriental and African Studies, London, October 27, 1989.

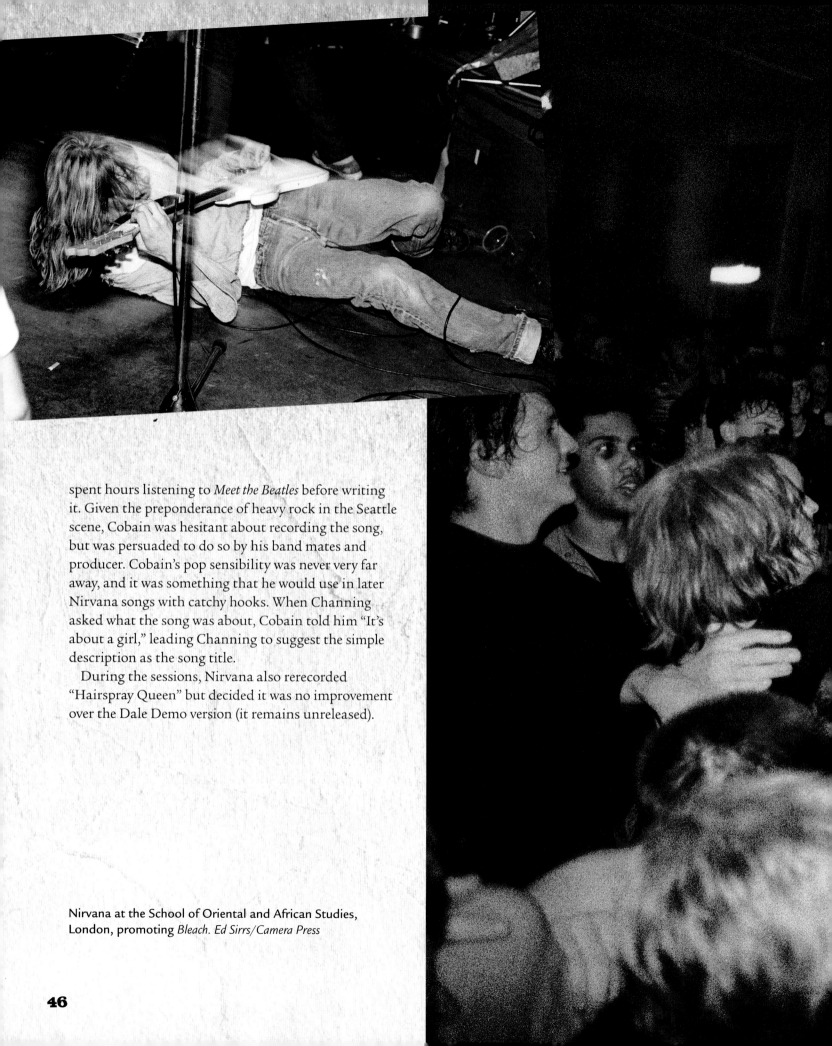

spent hours listening to *Meet the Beatles* before writing it. Given the preponderance of heavy rock in the Seattle scene, Cobain was hesitant about recording the song, but was persuaded to do so by his band mates and producer. Cobain's pop sensibility was never very far away, and it was something that he would use in later Nirvana songs with catchy hooks. When Channing asked what the song was about, Cobain told him "It's about a girl," leading Channing to suggest the simple description as the song title.

During the sessions, Nirvana also rerecorded "Hairspray Queen" but decided it was no improvement over the Dale Demo version (it remains unreleased).

Nirvana at the School of Oriental and African Studies, London, promoting *Bleach. Ed Sirrs/Camera Press*

Left: Flyer, Vera, Groningen, the Netherlands, November 2, 1989. *Middle:* Flyer, Petőfi Csarnok, Budapest, Hungary, November 21, 1989. *Right:* Nirvana released the *Blew* EP in December 1989. It was planned as promotion for an autumn 1989 European tour, but after this plan was scrapped, the EP was released exclusively in Great Britain. *Opposite:* Kurt Cobain in mid-air at Lamefest UK, Astoria, London, December 3, 1989. *Steve Double/Camera Press*

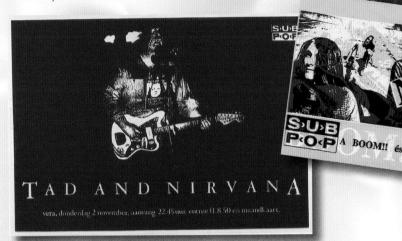

KURT'S TOP 50 ALBUMS

THE FROGS

It's Only Right and Natural (Homestead, 1989)
Back when flat-out weirdo visionaries were as likely to pop out of the indie rock scene as was a Superchunk or Buffalo Tom, the Frogs were a magnificent duo that escaped easy explanation and challenged the limits of humor while mesmerizing ears with beautiful psychedelic indie-folk rock on record and a live act of noise and heaviness that could stand arm hairs on end. The Frogs blindsided in-the-know audiences by following a forgettable debut with this amazing second album of "are they kidding or not?" gay-themed and gutter-romancing (and, to a great degree, funny-bone tickling) glam-folk that must be heard to be fully appreciated. And that's just a short intro to a career that defied logic and wooed the famous. R.I.P. Dennis Fleming. *AE*

Another song, "Big Long Now" (also named by Channing), would also remain unreleased at the time; Cobain felt they'd already recorded enough "slow, heavy" songs for the album (it was later released on *Incesticide*). The Dale Demo versions of "Paper Cuts" and "Floyd the Barber" were remixed for inclusion on the album, as was "Love Buzz." The U.S. and U.K. versions of the albums had slightly different song selections: the U.S. version had "Love Buzz," while the U.K. had "Big Cheese." A later CD release offered both, along with another Dale Demo number, "Downer."

Nirvana began extending their reach beyond Washington State, playing their first out-of-town gigs at the Portland, Oregon, club Satyricon, on January 6 and 21, 1989. In February, Nirvana traveled to California; while driving around San Francisco, signs urging IV drug users to "Bleach Your Works" as a way of stopping the spread of the AIDS virus gave the band the idea to call their upcoming album *Bleach* (among other titles,

Remains of a guitar smashed
by Kurt Cobain at the Astoria,
London, December 3, 1989.
Christie's/Bridgeman

KURT'S TOP 50 ALBUMS

PJ HARVEY

Dry (Too Pure, 1992)

While not as raw, crushing, or beautifully desperate as her sophomore album, *Rid of Me* (1993, Island), Polly Jean Harvey's debut full-length (sometimes credited to the PJ Harvey Trio) is packed with faster, more traditionally heavy indie rock marked with Harvey's unmistakable hush-to-a-howl vocals and infectious guitar work. *Dry* would inaugurate a long and very special discography that continues to influence and garner the utmost respect. *AE*

Flyer, East Ballroom, Husky Union Building, University of Washington, Seattle, Washington, January 6, 1990. Cobain and Novoselic destroyed so much gear during this show that they were banned for life from all University of Washington venues.

Cobain had been considering the more nihilistic *Too Many Humans*). There was also now a second guitarist in the band. Everman had been added to the group to help fill out the sound; as a new member, he was credited as a guitarist on *Bleach*, even though he doesn't actually appear on the record.

The band's next project was recording a track for *Hard to Believe*, a KISS tribute compilation released in August 1990 in the United States on Seattle-based C/Z Records. C/Z was run by Skin Yard member Daniel House, who had previously arranged to use "Mexican Seafood" from the Dale Demo on C/Z's EP compilation *Teriyaki Asthma Vol. 1*, released in August 1989.

Nirvana decided to record "Do You Love Me" from the KISS album *Destroyer*, arranging a session at Evergreen State College, which Greg Babior, a Nirvana fan and a musician himself, produced as part of a school project. The exact date of the session is unknown, beyond the fact it was in the spring (Babior also thinks there may have two sessions, one for recording, one for mixing).

It was Nirvana's first time in a 24-track studio, but they didn't take advantage of the setup. Indeed, there was a remarkable lack of seriousness about the whole endeavor—no rehearsal, the band simply listened to KISS's original track while on the way to the session, sharing a gallon jug of wine between them. Perhaps as a result, "Do You Love Me" comes across as more of a novelty record, especially due to its squalling "harmony" vocal by Novoselic. But the band also recorded an early version of "Dive" at the session, into which they put considerably more effort. The lyrics were unfinished, but musically the song already had a commanding presence, brooding during the verses, and building to a booming, climactic chorus. This early version was later released on *With the Lights Out*.

KURT'S TOP 50 ALBUMS

SONIC YOUTH

Daydream Nation (Blast First, 1988)

In sound and impact, the downright best record by a band whose discography has no shortage of influential and exhilarating titles. Sonic Youth's double-album masterstroke, *Daydream Nation*, is the consummation of an artistic vision quest that intensifies and hones the band's signature post-hardcore/proto–indie rock/experimental rock sound across an ascending arc defined by three years and three albums: 1985's *Bad Moon Rising*, 1986's *EVOL*, and 1987's *Sister*. *Daydream Nation* ranks alongside Hüsker Dü's *Zen Arcade* (1984), Dinosaur Jr's *You're Living All Over Me* (1987), the Pixies' *Surfer Rosa* (1988), and My Bloody Valentine's *Isn't Anything* (1988) for lighting the fuse of inspired underground and indie noise-rock that would continue until the end of the 1990s. AE

June 1989 proved an important month for Nirvana. On June 3, they signed their first contract with Sub Pop (backdated to January 1): a one-year contract, with two one-year options, offering $600 for the first album, $12,000 for the second, and $24,000 for third. Up to that point, Sub Pop hadn't signed contracts with their bands, but they'd drawn one up at Cobain and Novoselic's insistence, a sign of both men's growing ambitions.

Bleach was also released in June. The official release date was June 15, but early copies were on sale on June 9 at Sub Pop's first "Lame Fest," a concert held at Seattle's historic Moore Theatre, featuring Mudhoney, TAD, and Nirvana. It was the largest-scale event Sub Pop had yet hosted and the biggest stage Nirvana had so far played on; the band ended their set with Cobain leaping into Channing's drum kit, then waving goodbye as he left the stage, his guitar still tangled up in his hair.

Thirteen days later, Sub Pop sent the band out on their first U.S. tour, which began June 22 at the Covered Wagon Saloon in San Francisco. Attendance

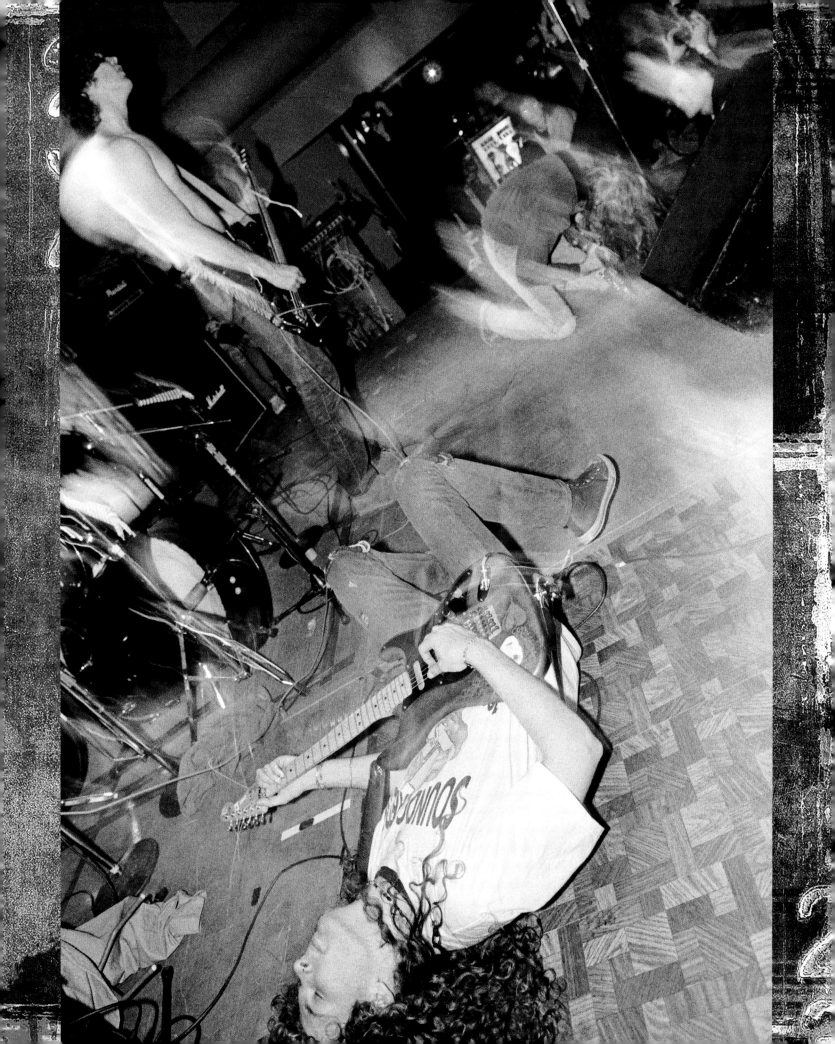

at the shows varied, and payment was equally variable; sometimes there was only enough money to pay for gas to get to the next show. The band slept rough, never able to afford a hotel. Cobain also had a longstanding, painful stomach problem, never properly diagnosed, which inevitably began flaring up on the band's tours. "And once he got sick, it would make everyone miserable," Everman observed.

On July 13, the band played a show at Maxwell's in Hoboken, New Jersey. Sonic Youth's Thurston Moore and Kim Gordon were in attendance and suitably impressed. Moore later memorably described the band to *Rolling Stone* as looking like "the *Children of the Corn* . . . total backwoods freaks." More importantly, Gordon passed on word about the band to Mark Kates, head of DGC's promotions department (Sonic Youth

Nirvana plays an in-store gig at Rough Trade Records, San Francisco, California, Valentine's Day, 1990. Members of TAD joined in, with Cobain playing while riding on Tad Doyle's shoulders. *Jay Blakesberg. Below:* Flyer, Legends, Tacoma, Washington, January 20, 1990. *Artist: Ryan Loiselle*

Left: Flyer, Pine Street Theatre, Portland, Oregon, February 9, 1990. *Middle:* Flyer, Cattle Club, Sacramento, California, February 12, 1990. *Right:* Flyer, Kennel Club, San Francisco, California, Valentine's Day, 1990. *Below:* Flyer, Bogart's, Long Beach, California, February 16, 1990.

KURT'S TOP 50 ALBUMS

THE KNACK

Get the Knack (Capitol, 1979)

The Knack's 1979 debut sideswiped radio and the music industry with its leadoff single, "My Sharona," and quickly raced up the charts. The most successful from-the-ground-up power-pop album of all time, *Get the Knack* went gold within thirteen days of release and diverted major-label attention from disco and album-oriented rock, the two areas previously subject to feeding frenzies and payola scandals in the late 1970s. *Get the Knack* is a punchy, unbelievably catchy, and somewhat sleazy album that seemed tailor-made for automobile, as opposed to home, enjoyment. *AE*

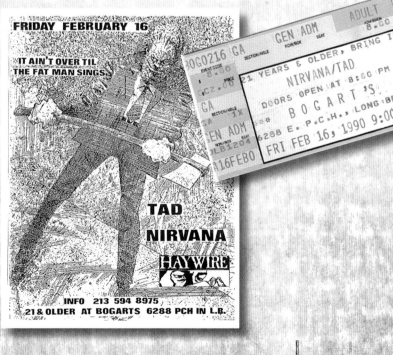

had recently signed with DGC, an imprint of Geffen Records), telling him, "The next band you sign should be Nirvana."

But Nirvana was still going through growing pains, evidenced by the progressively strained relations between Cobain and Everman. By the time the band reached New York City, the unhappiness was obvious to all, though contradictory stories explain what happened next. In one account, Cobain decided Everman was out of the band, but only told Novoselic; in another, Everman decided he would quit, but only told Channing. It was Cobain who ended up bringing the matter to a head, announcing after a July 18 show at New York's Pyramid club that the tour was over.

In later interviews, Cobain attributed the split with Everman to "musical differences." While there was some truth to the statement, a larger factor was probably Cobain's need to have complete dominance of the band. Everman had hoped to contribute to the band's songwriting, only to be shot down by Cobain. As he told the band's biographer, Michael Azerrad, "Basically, anybody besides Kurt or Krist is kind of disposable. At the end of the day, Kurt could get in front of any bass player and any drummer and play his songs and it's not going to sound that much different." Nor was he unhappy about leaving the band; when he was dropped off at home when the band arrived back in Seattle, he felt a great sense of relief. Typically, he wasn't told he was out of the band; he simply wasn't contacted again.

The following month, Cobain and Novoselic became involved in what could have been an interesting ongoing side project when Mark Lanegan and Mark Pickerel, singer and drummer, respectively, in the band

Top: Flyer, Iguana's, Tijuana, Mexico, February 17, 1990.
Middle and Bottom: Flyer, Cabaret Metro, Chicago, Illinois, April Fools' Day, 1990.

the Screaming Trees, approached them about forming a blues band. Lanegan and Pickerel were fans of legendary blues musician Huddie "Leadbelly" Ledbetter and knew that Cobain and Novoselic were as well. Everyone was excited about doing something new and different, quite unlike the grungy rock of the Seattle scene, and the four musicians spent two rehearsals listening to cassettes and picking out songs to do.

A recording session was booked at Reciprocal on August 20, with Endino producing. But there was a strange dynamic at the session; both Cobain and Lanegan were the dominant forces in their own groups, but now, working with each other, they kept that drive in check. No one pushed to be in charge, with the result being that no one really seemed to be "running the show," as Endino put it. Nonetheless, the musicians recorded a strong version of "Where Did You Sleep Last Night" with Lanegan on lead vocals, and a rollicking "Ain't It a Shame" with Cobain on lead vocals, both of which were considered for single release under a name Pickerel suggested, the Jury. But the single never happened and only "Where Did You Sleep Last Night" was released at the time, on Lanegan's solo debut *The Winding Sheet*, issued in May 1990 on Sub Pop (Nirvana would later perform a riveting version of the song as a set closer when they appeared on MTV's *Unplugged* in November 1993). "Ain't It a Shame" would later be released on *With the Lights Out*, along with the other tracks recorded at the session: the lugubrious instrumental "Grey Goose" and a poignant rendition of "They Hung Him on a Cross," featuring Cobain on lead vocals.

Soon after the Jury sessions, Nirvana went back into the studio for a session of their own. European dates were being scheduled for the fall and Sub Pop wanted an EP ready for the tour. The session was set up at

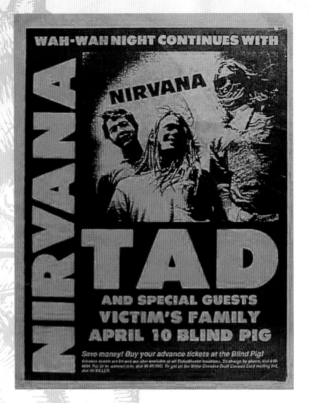

Above: Flyer, Blind Pig, Ann Arbor, Michigan, April 10, 1990. *Opposite:* Dressed in a dress, Cobain plays his guitar. *Steve Double/S.I.N./Alamy*

The Music Source in Seattle, which primarily catered to commercial clients but recorded rock bands in the evenings and on weekends. They also worked with a new producer, Steve Fisk, another Evergreen student, who had worked at KAOS and been in numerous bands (including two with Bruce Pavitt), and who had produced the Screaming Trees, Soundgarden, and Calvin Johnson's band, Beat Happening, among others.

The exact dates for the sessions aren't known, but they're believed to have been in September. Backing tracks and scratch vocals were laid down for five songs during the first session, with final vocals and overdubs done on two songs at the next session. The new songs showed the band moving further away from the sludgy territory of the Dale Demo and *Bleach*, with a decided pop undercurrent—something that helped disguise the unrelenting lyrical negativity: "Stain" has Cobain castigating a loser in the sole verse, only to reveal that the "loser" is himself in the chorus; "Even in His

Youth" castigates another lifelong failure; "Been a Son" bemoans the fate of those born girls instead of boys; "Polly" is an unsettling first-person portrait of a rapist. The mood only lightens on "Token Eastern Song" (so named for its melodic Middle Eastern groove, à la "Love Buzz"), though the chorus line, believed to be "Hold it in your gut," could possibly refer to Cobain's stomach woes.

"Stain" and "Been a Son" were the only songs completed. Fisk had Cobain doubling his vocals and guitar on the first song, and harmonizing his vocals on the second, giving them a buoyancy that Nirvana's music had previously lacked; indeed, while listening to the final mix of "Been a Son," Cobain, Novoselic, and Fisk were so excited that they climbed on a table to dance in celebration. The songs would appear on the *Blew* EP released that fall overseas, which also featured "Blew" and "Love Buzz," the latter track not

initially available on the non-U.S. version of *Bleach*. The remaining songs were later released on *With the Lights Out*.

A brief U.S. tour from September 28 to October 13 featured Ben Shepherd on second guitar, but Shepherd advised the band they'd be better off staying a three-piece (Shepherd then joined Soundgarden, and Nirvana eventually took on a second guitarist, Pat Smear, in 1993). While in Colorado, Cobain purchased a used 12-string Stella acoustic guitar for $32.21 that he would soon put to good use on "Polly" and "Something in the Way."

Then Nirvana set off on their first overseas tour, which ran October 23 to December 3, with thirty-seven shows in nine countries. Nirvana shared headlining duties with TAD and also toured with a live sound mixer and a tour manager. There was much anticipation about the tour. U.K. music weekly *Sounds*

KURT'S TOP 50 ALBUMS

THE SAINTS

"Know Your Product" b/w "Security" (EMI/Harvest, 1978)
The first punk rock band outside of the United States to publicly release material (1976's "I'm Stranded" b/w "No Time"), the Saints beat the Clash, Buzzcocks, Sex Pistols, and Damned at their own traditional punk rock game and then bested the post-punk movement by incorporating horns and R&B influences, as is heard best on this, the second single (and leadoff track) from their second album, *Eternally Yours*. AE

Above: Flyer, Pyramid Club, New York City, April 26, 1990. *Opposite:* Kurt Cobain smashes his guitar at the Pyramid Club, New York City. *Steve Double/Camera Press*

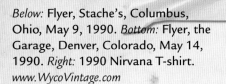

featured both groups on the cover of their October 21 issue, with the headline "Tad & Nirvana: Grabbing American by the Balls."

Novoselic wrecked some of the tour's rental gear at the very show (October 23 in Newcastle) when he slammed his bass through an amp because he was dissatisfied with the sound. Other shows were equally raucous; when Cobain felt the band's London debut show, October 27 at the School for Oriental and African Studies, needed an extra jolt of drama, he set off a fire extinguisher at the end of the set (he later said the show was his favorite of the tour).

But the band took a different tack on radio. On October 26, they taped a radio session for *The John Peel Show* in London (which aired November 22), performing "Love Buzz," "About a Girl," "Polly," and "Spank Thru," and on November 1, in the Netherlands, they made

LiLiPUT

KURT'S TOP 50 ALBUMS

KLEENEX/LiLiPUT

"anything by"

(Off Course/Rough Trade, 1978–1983)
Forced by a certain tissue-issuing corporate giant
to change their name, this Swiss, all-female post-
punk band had an idiosyncratic take on the genre
that veered from focused Slits-like dub-funk to
flailing madness to brittle, barely together shambles
and many points between. A favorite of the Pacific
Northwest indie-rock scenes that were not Seattle
(i.e., Portland and Olympia), Kleenex/LiLiPUT
enjoyed a comprehensive reissue their discography
across two CDs on the Kill Rock Stars label in 2001.
The band were contemporaneous of the U.K.'s
better-known Raincoats, hence no surprise that said
band's self-titled debut is next on Cobain's list. *AE*

Above: Flyer, Melody Ballroom, Portland, Oregon, August
23, 1990, and Moore Theatre, Seattle, Washington,
August 24, 1990. *Below:* Flyer, Hollywood Palladium,
Hollywood, California, August 17, 1990. Nirvana opened
several shows for Sonic Youth during their tour in support
of the release of *Goo.*

a live appearance on *Nozems-a-Gogo* for VPRO Radio,
performing "Love Buzz," "Dive," and "About a Girl."
The song selection emphasized Nirvana's pop side;
though they were wild on stage, radio appearances
allowed listeners to hear just how catchy Nirvana's
songs really were.

For the rest of the month, there were only four days
off. As on Nirvana's first U.S. tour, crowds varied from a
handful to packed houses, and sleeping arrangements
were similarly erratic. By the end of the month, everyone
was worn down, Cobain in particular. When Bruce
Pavitt and Jonathan Poneman arrived to meet the bands
in Rome on November 27, they were met with a hostile
reception from the tired, hungry, cold, and sick musicians.

Cobain finally snapped at that evening's show, when
he became frustrated with the sound equipment. Ten
songs into the set, he began smashing his guitar during

Left: Remnant of one of Krist Novoselic's basses from a Los Angeles show. *Kevin Estrada. Below and Opposite:* Band portraits with drummer Chad Channing, Novoselic, and Cobain. *Charles Peterson*

a performance of "Spank Thru," then climbed a speaker cabinet and threatened to jump. Though he came down after a few seconds, backstage he broke down in tears and announced he was quitting. The following day, Poneman arranged for him and Cobain to travel by train to the tour's next stop in Switzerland to give him a break from the crowded van. Unfortunately, Cobain's passport was stolen while he slept, leaving another mess to sort out.

A final show on December 3 at London's Astoria Theatre, billed as another Lame Fest, also featured Mudhoney. While no one in Nirvana rated their performance very highly ("It stunk," was Novoselic's blunt assessment), others recalled it quite differently. Journalist Keith Cameron, who would go on write extensively about Nirvana, told the band's biographer, Michael Azerrad, that Nirvana "was the most amazing band I'd ever seen." Anton Brookes, the band's U.K.

new view music productions

proudly presents

SONIC YOUTH

WITH VERY SPECIAL GUESTS

NIRVANA

AND

STP ALL AGES

MONDAY
AUG 20

8:00pm

$14.50 advance
$16. at the door

TICKETS ARE ALSO AVAILABLE AT THE BEAT RECORDS (33rd St. & Folsom Blvd.)

415/762-BASS
916/923-BASS

THE CREST

1013 K STREET - SACRAMENTO, CA.

INFO:(916) 442-3106

Flyer, Crest Theatre,
Sacramento, California,
August 20, 1990.

Above: Nirvana released its second, non-album single, "Sliver"/"Dive," in September 1990. *Right:* Poster, Motor Sports International Garage, Seattle, Washington, September 22, 1990. This was the only show that drummer Dan Peters played. Dave Grohl came to the show to see the band play. *Artist: Jim Blanchard*

publicist, also rated the show highly, noting it as the moment when audiences began to regard Nirvana, not Mudhoney, as the Next Big Thing in rock.

There was little activity for the rest of month; Cobain contributed backing vocals to "Down in the Dark" during sessions for Lanegan's *The Winding Sheet* album, and Novoselic married his girlfriend at the end of the month. Nirvana returned to Reciprocal on January 2 and 3, 1990, spending ten hours working on the song "Sappy." It was something of a step back for Nirvana, midtempo and not terribly compelling. Cobain apparently agreed, as Nirvana recorded the song three more times without completing a version that he was satisfied with. This early version was later released on *Sliver: The Best of the Box.*

A nine-date West Coast tour in February with TAD showed off the band's newfound prowess. And there were now more than just fans in the audience. After

Nirvana performs at Motorsports International Garage in Seattle. *Charles Peterson/Corbis*

Nirvana performs at Motorsports International Garage in Seattle. *Charles Peterson/Corbis*

KURT'S TOP 50 ALBUMS

THE RAINCOATS

The Raincoats (Rough Trade, 1979)
In one of Cobain's great altruistic moves (there were many), he coerced DGC to reissue the Raincoats' discography in 1993 after meeting the band's Ana da Silva as she was tending a cousin's London antique shop around the corner from Rough Trade Records. The Raincoats' self-titled debut is unlike any post-punk album of the genre's heyday, at times sounding like dismantled pop reassembled incorrectly and at other points gelling into fantastic catchiness. Yet it holds steady as their most challenging work, as the brief discography predating their decade-long hiatus beginning in the early 1980s tends more toward traditional fare. The band reunited to much acclaim in 1993 following Cobain's generosity. *AE*

YOUNG
MARBLE
GIANTS

COLOSSAL YOUTH

KURT'S TOP 50 ALBUMS

YOUNG MARBLE GIANTS
Colossal Youth (Rough Trade, 1980)
Continuing Cobain's love of eccentric U.K. post-punk with a lady's touch, Young Marble Giants (Cardiff, Wales) were, along with The Vaselines, cited by the singer/guitarist as his all-time favorite band. The band's sole album holds only the aforementioned common denominators with the two previously covered bands, as, once again, a contemporary in sound and era simply does not exist. Drummer-less and with a major emphasis on simplicity, this album is more at home with Eno's pop works (a huge influence); the DIY movement that was coalescing at the same time and in the same region (early Scritti Politti, Orange Juice, Television Personalities, etc.); and, though not the stretch it may first seem, with early industrialists like Cabaret Voltaire (with whom they toured). *AE*

Sonic Youth's recommendation, DGC's Mark Kates made a point of seeing Nirvana's February 14 show in San Francisco. Amid this growing interest, Sub Pop was anxious to get Nirvana back in the studio to record a second album, and booked sessions with producer Butch Vig at Smart Studios in Madison, Wisconsin, in April.

Prior to the trip, Cobain worked on another project of his own, arranging to shoot some videos with an eye toward preparing for a tape the band could sell on tour. He asked Evergreen student Jon Snyder to direct, knowing that Snyder was not only a Nirvana fan but also had access to the college's television studio. Snyder readily agreed, and a shoot was set up for March 20. Greg Babior, who'd produced the "Do You Love Me"/"Dive" session, was brought in to do sound.

The resulting videos for "School," "Big Cheese," and "Floyd the Barber" featured live performances spliced with footage drawn from the extensive collection of material Cobain had videotaped during his hours of TV viewing. The footage used during "School" featured teen idols Leif Garrett, Kristy McNicol, and Shaun Cassidy, a subtle commentary on the phoniness of celebrity culture, while the footage used during "Big Cheese," taken from Benjamin Christensen's 1922 silent film *Häxan* ("The Witch"), was effective in creating an atmospheric mood. Though never officially released, the videos have been extensively bootlegged.

Most interesting was a song filmed during a sound check. "Lithium," which the band had yet to play live, was Kurt's most tuneful song since "About a Girl," and even in this rough, early stage, in a halting performance and without its final lyrics, it captivated the small crew working on the shoot. This was the song, not "School" or "Floyd the Barber," that pointed the way ahead. After spending years working to craft a distinctive voice, Cobain had at last found the winning formula.

New drummer Dave Grohl, Cobain, and Novoselic. Grohl played his first show with Nirvana on October 11, 1990, in Olympia, Washington. *AF archive/Alamy*

RADIO FRIENDLY UNIT SHIFTER

3. THE *NEVERMIND* YEARS

By Bob Gendron

Kurt Cobain goes aerial.
Charles Peterson/Time Life Pictures/Getty Images

Not since the sneering sounds and confrontational messages of Bob Dylan's anthemic "Like a Rolling Stone" had the world heard a song that caused such profound sea changes in music, pop culture, and public attitudes. And not since the Clash's *London Calling* had an album initiated seismic shifts that crossed into both public and political spheres, served as a rallying cry for the frustrations of a young generation, and stimulated dialog that emerged from the underground before rippling through the mainstream.

Nirvana's "Smells Like Teen Spirit" and major-label debut *Nevermind* accomplished both feats, infiltrating the commercial consciousness in ways antagonistic pioneers like the Sex Pistols and Public Enemy never achieved. In less than four months, the Seattle trio metamorphosed from an indie-rock buzz band to a household name that knocked Michael Jackson from atop the pop throne and forever stymied the skirt-chasing dreams of showbiz poseurs on both sides of the Atlantic. The group's January 11, 1992, performance on *Saturday Night Live*, then the primary medium for an artist to gain exposure to conservative mid-America and tens of millions without cable television, permanently altered the musical landscape. It was Generation X's equivalent to Elvis Presley's ballyhooed *Ed Sullivan Show* appearance decades earlier. There was no going back. Grunge, soon a catchphrase echoed everywhere from junior-high playgrounds to highbrow department stores, had broken. Alternative rock was no longer confined to dive-bar clubs, college radio stations, small press outlets, and in-the-know listeners.

Backstage passes.

This (r)evolution transpired without the aid of the Internet, the absence of which, ironically, helped make the groundswell possible by allowing for elements of surprise, anticipation, and community that are impossible in the information-overloaded twenty-first century. Unable to be seen on YouTube, shared on download sites, hyped on Twitter, liked on Facebook, streamed on Spotify, or sampled on Pandora, Nirvana came of age during an era in which social media constituted word-of-mouth recommendations, homemade fanzines, tape trading, local music publications, and conversations with neighborhood record-store clerks. Few, if any, insiders—even those closest to the band—foresaw the extent of the transformation wrought by three misfits Geffen Records executives hoped might sell 250,000 records at best.

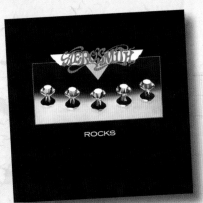

KURT'S TOP 50 ALBUMS

AEROSMITH

Rocks (Columbia, 1976)

Rocks was released as three years of constant touring began to pay off. Former regional hit "Dream On" shot into the Top 20 for eight weeks in early 1976 and the previous year's "Walk This Way" (from 1975's scorching *Toys in the Attic*) began climbing the charts in December to reach a January 1977 peak of No. 13. *Rocks* didn't send any of its tracks into the Top 20, but it did feature the eventual radio staple "Back in the Saddle" and the thick white funk of "Last Child." It's Aerosmith's grittiest affair to date—a sonic snapshot of the Toxic Twins reaching their functional threshold, right before the band's notorious unraveling commenced. *AE*

Above: **Kurt Cobain's 1953 Martin D-18 guitar, which he bought while on tour just before the release of** *Nevermind*. *Heritage Auctions. Opposite:* **Band portrait with Novoselic, Cobain, and Grohl.** *Kevin Estrada*

Left: Backstage pass. *Kevin Estrada. Below:* Tickets, Great Britain Tour, Fall 1990. *Opposite:* Band portrait with Novoselic, Cobain, and Grohl. *Kevin Estrada*

KURT'S TOP 50 ALBUMS

VARIOUS ARTISTS

What Is It? (What Records?, 1982)

This often-overlooked punk rock and early hardcore compilation (ten tracks, eight bands) on Los Angeles' What Records? is notable for featuring the first Germs recordings ("Forming" and "Round and Round"); the Eyes (pre–X DJ Bonebrake and pre–Go-Go's Charlotte Caffey); pre–Wall of Voodoo punk band the Skulls; the Dils' classic, "I Hate the Rich"; pre-Kaos (also included here) band the Controllers; an early Agent Orange track; and previously unreleased material by the Spastics. *AE*

"There was the sort of grass-roots hype on this band I can only compare to when I was a teenager and people said Bruce Springsteen was the best performer in the world," said Sub Pop cofounder Jonathan Poneman in a January 1992 *Musician* article by Chris Morris. "These three individuals represent their generation. It's a luck of timing: This band not only delivers the goods, they manage to capture the time."

Poneman is half-correct. Nirvana encapsulated its time, but the group's breakout owes less to the "good timing" reason cited by most critics, writers, and industry representatives who try to explain the hows and whys of the whirlwind success. Luck and timing are easy and convenient answers, but fail to account for why a host of other angst-ridden bands—Sonic Youth, Dinosaur Jr, Alice in Chains, Jane's Addiction, Soul Asylum, the Pixies—failed to hit the jackpot scored by Nirvana. They released major-label albums before *Nevermind* and were active during the same

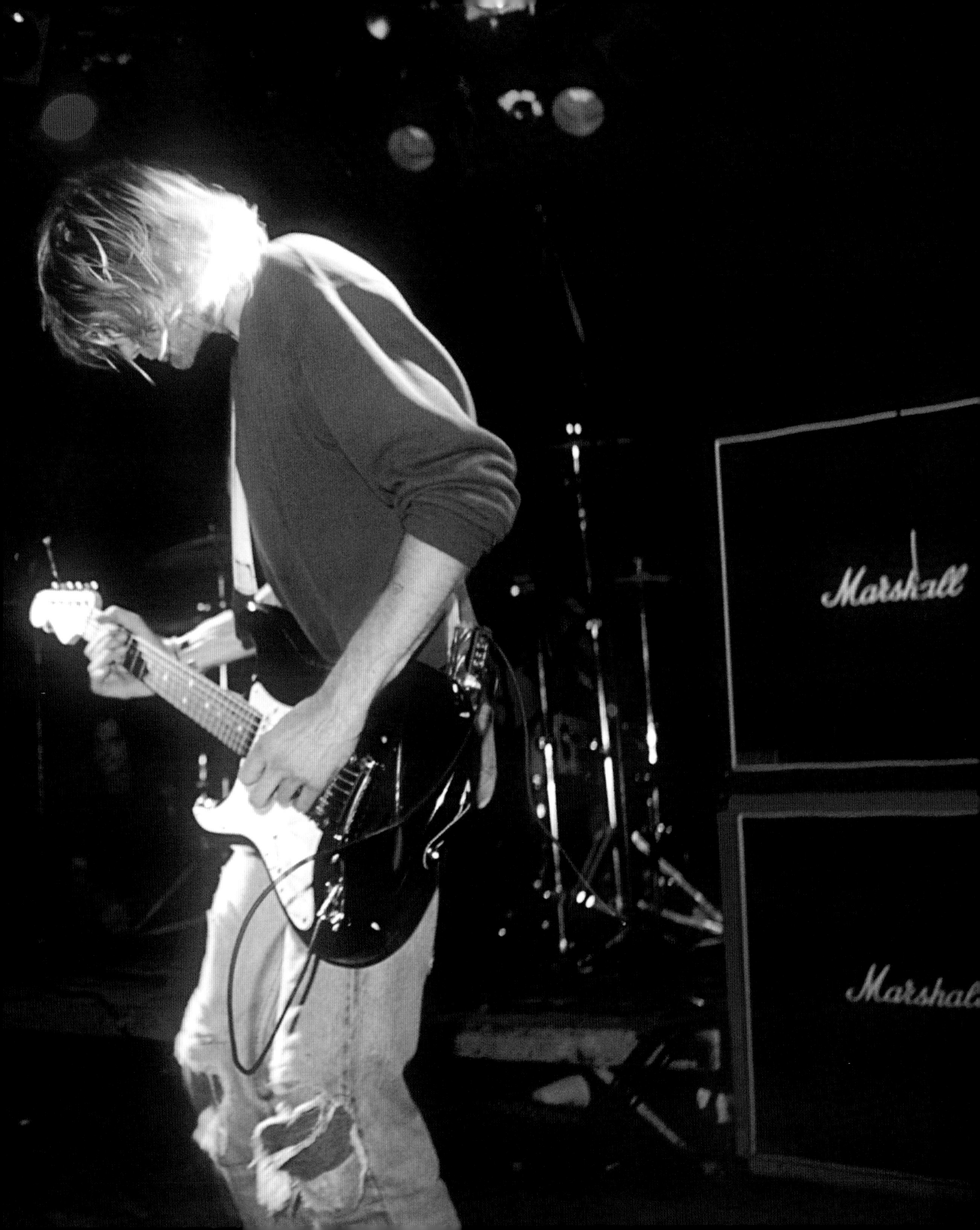
Marshall
Marshall

Previous, this spread, and following: Nirvana in concert. *Kevin Estrada*

period. Mudhoney, Soundgarden, and TAD also enter into any such discussion, as each Sub Pop peer received relatively similar treatment from the label's sarcastic promotion department.

The existence of Nirvana's contemporaries, as well as Lollapalooza's triumphant debut in summer 1991, give lie to the widely disseminated myth of *Nevermind* seemingly coming from nowhere, blowing up overnight, and vaporizing hedonistic Sunset Strip–bred rock in its wake. As it often is, the truth is more complicated, and owes to a conflux of intertwining factors, not the least of which involves the then-deplorable state of popular music.

After peaking in the late 1980s, blow-dried metal breathed on life support in 1991, with Warrant touting the subgenre's last hit and regularly played video: 1990's *Cherry Pie*. Reagan-era standbys Mötley Crüe, Poison, Cinderella, and Dokken withered from personnel

issues. Bon Jovi took a hiatus. Disappointing sales also indicate the heyday had run its course. No rock album reached number-one on the *Billboard* charts in 1990, a year governed by easy-listening fluff (Wilson Phillips), placid synthpop (Depeche Mode), quiet storm R&B (Keith Sweat, Johnny Gill), soundtracks (*Ghost, Pretty Woman, Young Guns II*), and, most prominently, toothless kiddie rap (MC Hammer, Vanilla Ice).

Primarily ignorant of the underground artists swaying college-aged listeners and filling 900- to

Opposite and Above: Cobain communes with his guitar. *Kevin Estrada. Left:* Flyer, Satyricon, Portland, Oregon, December 31, 1990. The bar gave out free bottles of champagne to celebrate the new year, and during the opening band's set, bottles were thrown against the wall behind the stage, leaving shattered glass covering the stage. When Nirvana came onstage, Novoselic swept away some of the glass, then took his shoes off to play.

KILL the GRATEFUL DEAD

PUNKS NOT DEAD

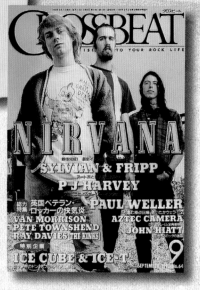

Kurt Cobain's self-styled Punk Duck shirt, which he wore for the cover photo shoot for the Japanese magazine *Crossbeat. Heritage Auctions*

GREEN R.E.M.

KURT'S TOP 50 ALBUMS

R.E.M.
Green (Warner Bros., 1988)

To properly frame the honesty and lack of airs behind this list, it's important to note something about R.E.M.: The now-defunct band continues to endure a raw deal when it comes to their credit for the American underground's development and fruition in the 1980s, for no better reason than their avoidance of ear-shattering guitar distortion, aggro-militant rhythms, bowel-excavating bass, blatant negativity, or other sonic and aesthetic announcements of aggression or alienation. Turning down bigger offers in favor of Warner Bros.' promise of 100 percent creative control, the band left longtime label I.R.S. Records and went all over the map in a very non-R.E.M. fashion for much of their Warners debut, an album that gave the band their first real U.S. hit with "Stand" but also a much larger stage from which to tackle sociopolitical concerns (e.g., the dirge-y first single "Orange Crush"). *AE*

SUB-POP RECORDING ARTISTS FROM Seattle:

NIRVANA

AT: BRONX 10030-102 ST.
WITH GUESTS: ZERO TOLERANCE
$6 IN ADVANCE AT SOUND CONNECTION AND SOUTHSIDE SOUND $7 MEMBERS $7.50 NON-MEMBERS AT THE DOOR
DOORS OPEN @ 9:00
TUESDAY, MARCH 5TH

FM88 CJSR·FM • Cable 104.7

Flyer, the Bronx, Edmonton, Alberta, Canada, March 4, 1991.

THE GOOD, THE BAD AND THE UGLY
LIVE SHOWS AT THE BRONX
141
FROM SEATTLE SUB POP RECORDING ARTISTS
NIRVANA
PLUS GUESTS
ZERO TOLERANCE
TUESDAY, MAR 5/91
DOORS OPEN 9 PM
BRONX
10030 - 102 ST.
$ 6.00/ADVANCE
$ 7.00/MEMBERS AT DOOR
$ 7.50/GUESTS AT DOOR

Left: Nirvana on the cover of *Rolling Stone*, April 16, 1992. *Right:* Flyer, Commodore Ballroom, Vancouver, British Columbia, Canada, March 8, 1991.

1,100-capacity clubs like Chicago's Metro and Boston's Paradise, the old guard was ready for a shakeup. Mainstream tastes became increasingly vapid as major labels, getting fat off profits from higher-priced CDs, milked the latter for all their worth. Middling, corporate boardroom-planned affairs from Paula Abdul, MC Hammer, Boyz II Men, Michael Bolton, Natalie Cole, Genesis, Bryan Adams, Color Me Badd, Van Hagar, and Mariah Carey dominated Top 10 charts for months on end. Garth Brooks reigned as the uncontested superstar. The slickness, bloat, and prepackaged emotions mirrored the cocaine-addled, me-first 1980s. Darker and distressed, the early 1990s— pockmarked by the Gulf War, Rodney King beating, unemployment problems, and Bush's reversal on tax increases—cried out for grit and substance.

When Skid Row's thrashing *Slave to the Grind* crash-landed at number one in July, it spoke as many volumes about the public's pent-up demand for aggressive rock as it did the accuracy of the new SoundScan system, which measured record sales by piece count rather

than by the prior phone-in technique subject to biases, errors, and lies. Metallica and Guns N' Roses finally bridged the rock void in the early fall with blockbusters. But neither seized the zeitgeist and both bands, fairly or not, remained tethered to a prior era.

Rock's extensive drought confirmed audiences wanted something different, something onto which they could latch, something genuine that relayed the discontent, confusion, and exasperation of growing up amid a recession and end of the Cold War. The sons and daughters of baby boomers craved their own music, not that of their parents, and certainly not mainstream-pushed pop whose very existence seemed to treat audiences as inferior, stupid, and gullible. They yearned for something played by musicians more relevant than bigger-than-life stars depicted bare-chested on centerfold-style pinup posters.

Ohio-born Dave Grohl worshipped no such false idols. His world changed at thirteen when, chaperoned by his cousin Tracy, the hyperactive teenager attended

a Naked Raygun concert and instantly fell in love with punk. Grohl spent the next few years playing drums in a series of bands before dropping out of high school and joining Washington, D.C., hardcore legends Scream. At the behest of the Melvins, Kurt Cobain and Chris Novoselic went to see Scream play in San Francisco in 1990.

The pair had recently split with drummer Chad Channing, whose mellow personality, drumming technique, and musical interests didn't jive with those of his former band mates. He also wanted to contribute songs to the band, a wish Cobain refused to grant. Having entertained a revolving assembly of drummers, Cobain and Novoselic were smitten with Grohl. Several weeks later, Scream's bassist abandoned the tour, stranding the drummer in Los Angeles and leaving him in need of a band.

"I called Chris, and said hello," Grohl later told *Melody Maker* writer Everett True, adding that he was initially rebuffed on his offer to join the group since Mudhoney's Dan Peters had allegedly taken the drummer's role. "They called back that night and said, maybe it's a good idea that you come up and play." In the 2013 Mudhoney documentary, *I'm Now*, Peters recalls that Grohl was hanging out at a Nirvana photo shoot in which he, Cobain, and Novoselic were the subjects. In a scenario that had previously played out on the Nirvana drum stool, Peters had been sacked without knowing it.

Grohl's simple approach and pounding, hard-hitting mechanics suited Nirvana's style. But his other skills turned the band into a powerhouse. Grohl's violent, economical energy and intense aggression, combined with his harmonizing abilities, gave the band countless new dimensions, including a more pronounced professionalism. Advanced from its earlier, scrappier style, Nirvana now sounded like it could conquer the universe.

As if a sign from above, Grohl's first show with Nirvana, in Olympia on October 11, 1990, sold out

Opposite: **Cobain with Fender Mustang guitar.**
KMazur/WireImage/Getty Images

Top: Flyer, O.K. Hotel, Seattle, Washington, April 17, 1991. *Middle:* Flyer, Gothic Theatre, Englewood, Colorado, June 10, 1991. *Bottom:* 1991 Nirvana *Nevermind* Tour T-shirt. *www.WycoVintage.com*

almost instantaneously. The sheer force of his playing broke a snare drum; the power went out twice. By all accounts triumphant, the concert represents the start of the best period in the group's brief history—a stretch that would end a year later when the pressures of juggling fame, expectations, drug addictions, depression, and love interests reshaped the band's working dynamic and forced members out of their comfort zones. In just more than a year's time, Nirvana would progress from conducting anything-goes interviews with college newspapers to getting hounded by every major press outlet in the United States and Europe.

Grohl's impact carried over to the studio. While he admittedly played Chad Channing's parts on *Nevermind*, his hardcore background and emulation of Led Zeppelin icon John Bonham put him on an entirely different level. His thundering and bashing also netted a much-overlooked consequence: Nirvana not only sounded bigger and heavier with Grohl on the drum stool—it sounded poppier, catchier, and more spacious and accessible, all crucial to any artist's mainstream acceptance. Outside of the Pixies and, to an extent, Dinosaur Jr, none of Nirvana's peers boasted such a lethal combination of traits. And none selected the team of Butch Vig and Andy Wallace to produce and mix their album.

Accustomed to working with small Midwestern acts such Killdozer, Die Kreuzen, and Urge Overkill, and intimately familiar with the indie aesthetic, Vig had previously recorded Nirvana with Channing behind the kit in April 1990 at Madison's Smart Studios. Initially, the eight tracks formulated at the sessions, including

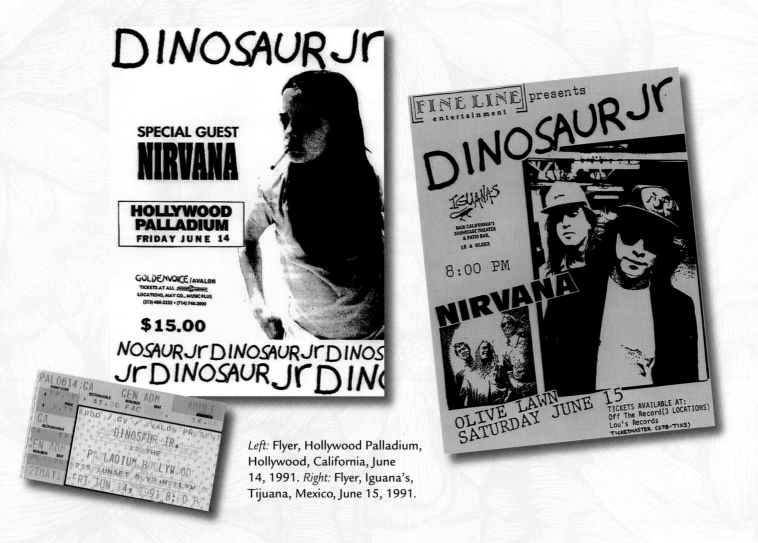

Left: Flyer, Hollywood Palladium, Hollywood, California, June 14, 1991. *Right:* Flyer, Iguana's, Tijuana, Mexico, June 15, 1991.

a cochlea-tingling cover of the Velvet Underground's "Here She Comes Now," were tagged for the group's sophomore Sub Pop album but became the bait with which the trio lured major labels. Five of the songs ended up on *Nevermind*, all but "Polly" improved by Grohl's battery of percussion. *Nevermind* marked Vig's virgin experience with a major-label release. His ear for pop melody and abrasive noise proved prophetic. The record stands as the 1990s version of AC/DC's *Back in Black*—a mega-selling, stadium-level benchmark that myriad bands attempted to copy, and asked producers to emulate, for years to come.

Strong albeit sleek, tuneful yet distorted, produced but raw and visceral, *Nevermind*'s sonic architecture ranks as importantly as any other detail associated with the album. Akin to the band's rise independent

KURT'S TOP 50 ALBUMS

SHONEN KNIFE
Burning Farm
(K Records cassette-only reissue, 1985)
The Japanese have always made better use of American culture than Americans, and the three ladies in Shonen Knife (translates to "Boy Knife") mixed up Phil Spector girl groups, garage rock, bubblegum pop, punk rock, and children's tunes. The trio began to lob this purposely simplistic meshwork back at the United States with K Records' ultra-limited cassette reissue of *Burning Farm*, their 1983 debut. Sub Pop included Shonen Knife on the game-changing *Sub Pop 100* compilation in 1986, and the band eventually saw major label action in the 1990s, but for the most part it doesn't beat this little album's innocent distillation of Western polarities. It should also be noted that the Knife were a massive influence on the Olympia, Washington, scene (Beat Happening, etc.) that revolved around K Records. *AE*

Casting call flyer, "Smells Like Teen Spirit" music video shoot, August 17, 1991. *Kevin Estrada*

Kurt Cobain wearing a wall hanging of Jesus at the "Smells Like Teen Spirit" music video shoot, August 17, 1991. He's playing his 1969 Fender Competition Mustang guitar.
Kevin Estrada

Hi Kev,

Thanks for the video - I looove it!
Here's some music. Hope you like ~~them~~ it
I'm proud of it!   well, write back soon

                    Love, your pal
                         kurdt

Letter from Cobain to Kevin Estrada, thanking him for his photography during the "Smells Like Teen Spirit" shoot. *Kevin Estrada*

KURT'S TOP 50 ALBUMS

THE SLITS

Typical Girls EP (Island/Antilles, 1979)
This is the extended 12-inch version of the Slits' "Typical Girls" single from their timeless 1979 debut album, *Cut*. Though active since 1976, and having provided support for early tours by the Clash, Buzzcocks, and Subway Sect, the band (Ari Up/vocals, Viv Albertine/guitar, Teresa Pollit/bass, and Siouxie and the Banshees' Budgie/drums) had been moving away from their punk roots for some time, and *Cut* is surely informed by dub reggae, funk, and R&B (with added effects by producer and noted British reggae legend Dennis Bovell), but it is the alternative versions on this EP, as well as the B-side cover of "Heard It Through the Grapevine," that really captured the band preparing for one of post-punk's more devoted headlong dives into dub. *AE*

of the Internet, it's largely a product of a bygone era. If *Nevermind* came out in the 2000s, odds are against it sounding so dynamic, open, and explosive. The advent of MP3s, portable electronics, cell phones, and convenience over quality has coincided with a trend favoring compression, a production technique that increases loudness at the expense of squelching high and low frequencies. Producers weren't under such constraints in the early 1990s. Listening to music still often involved home stereos, and record labels didn't feel obliged to construct the loudest possible songs in order to attract radio programmers' attention.

Completed for approximately $130,000 (double the original budget) in seven weeks at Van Nuys' Sound City Studios, *Nevermind* benefits from Vig's decision to record the band live as a trio before adding guitars and revised vocals. The latter were also doubled, against Cobain's protestations. But the percussion is what sticks out. The studio's large room—along with ambient miking techniques, Vig's experience as a drummer, Grohl's drumhead-breaking strength, and the acquisition of an extremely heavy 6½x14-inch bell brass snare drum dubbed "The Terminator"—generated a monstrous bottom end and gut-slamming punch.

However controversial, Wallace shares credit in fine-tuning the overall results. Brought in by Geffen to mix given his pedigree with Slayer and Run-DMC, the engineer boosted the drums with equalization and blended samples. Entire songs were run through special-effects devices to smooth out and modernize the nakedness. While the music became more processed, it gained stereo separation as wide as a football field and balanced abrasive grit with radio-friendly slickness. Cobain lambasted the outcome.

"Looking back on the production of *Nevermind*, I'm embarrassed by it now," he told journalist Michael Azerrad in the book *Come As You Are*, published in 1993. "It's closer to a Mötley Crüe record than it is a punk rock record."

Tossing salt in the wound, ex-mate Channing went on record in the same publication, stating, "*Nevermind* isn't grunge. It's a freaking rock album. That's what happens when you get to the major labels. They want everything

Above: Flyer, Sir Henry's, Cork, Ireland, August 20, 1991. *Below:* Kurt Cobain grabs a nap before Nirvana's show at Sir Henry's, Cork, Ireland. *Ed Sirrs/Camera Press. Opposite:* Cobain awake and in action at Sir Henry's, Cork, Ireland. *Ed Sirrs/Camera Press*

The sticker on the guitar reads:

> VANDALISM:
> BEAUTIFUL AS A ROCK
> IN A COP'S FACE

NEVERMIND

by Jim DeRogatis

"I have always believed that rock 'n' roll comes down to myth. There are no 'facts,'" wrote the late, great Lester Bangs, a hero to the late, great Kurt Cobain. (The musician scribbled a letter to the dead rock critic in one of his Mead notebooks, and it was published posthumously in *Journals*.)

The myth about *Nevermind* is that it came out of nowhere—because that's how the music industry allegedly viewed both indie rock and Seattle—and exploded overnight in 1991, "the year punk broke." Nirvana instantly upended a flaccid music world that had given rock up for dead; suddenly, alternative rock was ascendant and the gold rush was on. Hello, "Smells Like Teen Spirit," goodbye (and good riddance), hair metal and Michael Jackson.

Punk had had a similarly dramatic impact in the mid-1970s, to be sure, with the Ramones, the Sex Pistols, and their peers inspiring a new generation of musicians making much harsher and less compromising sounds. But they soon were banished to the underground, confined to the world of DIY van tours, struggling indie labels, shithole clubs, tiny mom-and-pop record stores, self-published fanzines, and left-of-the-dial college radio stations lovingly described in Gina Arnold's *Route 666: On the Road to Nirvana* and Michael Azerrad's *Our Band Could Be Your Life*.

There, the sounds Kurt and the boys loved would have languished until they stormed the fortress of the music industry, climbed the daunting heights of the pop charts, and changed the world. Or until, as Arnold succinctly put it, "We won."

Yeah, well, sorta. The victory was a pyrrhic one at best, and short-lived. But even setting that aside, there are serious problems with this version of history. And Kurt, as dedicated a myth-buster as Lester, was the first to tell you that.

Released on September 24, 1991, *Nevermind* hardly was an overnight success: The build was slow but steady. In an era when many big names sold a million or more albums in week one, Nirvana took two months to reach platinum status of a million copies sold. And things only really exploded two months after that, on January 25, 1992, when the trio's major-label debut shot from No. 6 on the *Billboard* Top 200 Albums Chart to No. 1, dethroning *Dangerous* by the King of Pop (though his sales already were waning).

Rock had indeed been moribund throughout 1990, when not a single rock band hit No. 1 on the albums chart. But it bounced back in the eight months before Nirvana topped the chart, with R.E.M., Skid Row, Van Halen, Metallica, Guns N' Roses, and U2 all preceding *Nevermind* at No. 1 at various times in 1991.

Another factor behind Nirvana's chart success rarely mentioned was that it came shortly after the Christmas holidays—a period of sparse releases back in the days of physical product, and one which *Billboard*, in its article about the January 25 charts, characterized as tending "to include more fluky, ephemeral stuff, teen sensations (Tiffany, New Kids On The Block), flavor-of-the-month pop acts (Milli Vanilli, Vanilla Ice), TV spinoffs (*Miami Vice*, *The Simpsons*), and MTV-boosted movie soundtracks (*Dirty Dancing*, *Cocktail*)." The article added, "Part of the album's surge comes from the standard post-Christmas rush, when young buyers, on vacation and with Christmas money or gift certificates, hit the stores."

The thing about flukes is that no one ever really sees them coming, though many later claim they did. By late January, *Nevermind* was selling 300,000 copies a week, and sales would hone to that impressive number for quite some time. (The album would be certified ten times platinum, with sales of 10 million, in 1999.) But no one was more surprised than the folks at the band's label, Geffen Records. They had shipped a mere 46,000

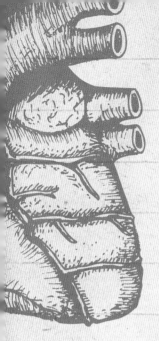

copies to stores throughout the United States the week of the disc's release, and they didn't anticipate having to restock it for quite some time. "Nirvana has outsold over the last two or three weeks U2, Hammer, Michael Jackson, Metallica: real big-name values," Geffen sales exec Eddie Gilreath told the *New York Times* in mid-January. "If you told me last year it would outsell U2, I'd probably die laughing."

If the music industry has never really been able to predict a hit, it always has known how to capitalize on one. *Nevermind* stayed at No. 1 longer than it might have thanks to Nirvana appearing on *Saturday Night Live* the following week, MTV fully embracing the video for "Smells Like Teen Spirit," and radio following suit—and all of that came about as the big-money star machine kicked into gear because of the quality of the music.

Nevermind was released by David Geffen Company (DGC) on September 24, 1991.

"[Nirvana bassist] Krist [Novoselic] says shit like, 'Nirvana didn't come to the public, the public came to Nirvana.' That's one of his favorites," the inimitable Courtney Love, a.k.a. the Widow Cobain, told me in 2002. "But that neglects the fact that [notorious independent record promoter] Jeff McCluskey sure as fuck got paid, and so did the rack jobbers, and so did the fucking handlers, and so did the guy in Thailand, and so did that guy, and so did that guy, and so did that guy! It was marketing money!"

As usual, La Love was exaggerating, but just a bit. Though both Krist and Kurt were prone to some sociological philosophizing about why *Nevermind* captured the public's imagination when it did—"In January 1990, George Bush had like an eighty-five percent approval rating, and in 1992 when *Nevermind* was happening, we elected this governor from Arkansas," Krist told me a year later. "Maybe it took until late 1992 for the 1990s to happen"—neither of them ever gave sole credit to the band's music. Nor did they ignore the role the industry played in pushing it. In fact, they were somewhat embarrassed and disgusted by that; witness the T-shirt slogan "Flower Sniffin', Kitty Pettin', Baby Kissin' Corporate Rock Whores."

Just as importantly, Nirvana never failed to mention that it had signed to Geffen in the first place because the label had become home to New York noise-rockers Sonic Youth in the summer of 1989. The band also was well aware that Hüsker Dü had issued their last two albums on a major label, Warner Bros., in 1986 and 1987, and that by 1990, that company and various subsidiaries were home to the Replacements, Jane's Addiction, the Flaming Lips, and Dinosaur Jr. The Butthole Surfers were recording for Capitol Records, Soul Asylum was on A&M, and the Pixies' albums for the English indie 4AD were distributed in the United States by Elektra. In fact, the Pixies, whose loud/quiet, noisy/melodic shifts were a big influence on Nirvana, released their last album, *Trompe le Monde*, the same day Nirvana dropped *Nevermind*.

When I asked Krist during that same 1993 interview why none of those bands had done what Nirvana did, he was stumped. Initially he just shrugged, but I pressed him. Mudhoney's classic "If I Think" from 1988's *Superfuzz*

Bigmuff EP was easily the anthemic equal of "Smells Like Teen Spirit," I said. Why didn't that band have the success that Nirvana did?

"Maybe it was the production," Novoselic finally concluded. "What 'If I Think' did was help to unite the Seattle scene. When that EP came out, it was a must-have, and those were magical times. *That* was the Seattle scene. When Mudhoney was playing and we were playing, and TAD and the Fluid. That was a little time in history that you can compare to the Liverpool scene, the Cavern Club. It was innocent. It wasn't exploited. Now look what it's come to. Everybody's older and wiser."

After *Nevermind*, the major labels did descend en masse on the indie-rock underground—with special emphasis on Seattle and, later, Chicago—signing every band possible with the hope of landing the post-Nirvana "next big thing." By 1993, most major American cities had a "New Rock Alternative" corporate radio station all too eager to help sell these new sounds, and MTV couldn't get enough of them (back when the station still actually aired music videos).

But this was no victory. Ultimately, much more crap than brilliance came from this feeding frenzy. For every group like the Melvins (for whom Kurt and Krist used to haul gear) or Eugenius (the new group started by Cobain's idol, Eugene Kelly, formerly of the Vaselines) that benefited, however briefly, from major-label money and marketing, there were at least three awful cookie-cutter wannabes like Bush, Stone Temple Pilots, Marcy Playground, and Sugar Ray. Cobain famously disdained even Pearl Jam as corporate sellouts, though whether or not he was right is a fight for another day.

"There are some bands out there now that would easily fit into the repertoire of, say, Rick Springfield or Phil Collins," a disgusted Krist told me. "But they're young, they dress kind of hip and modern, and they're called alternative. It's just bullshit. It's just exploitation."

Kurt was just as sickened by the "alternative-rock explosion" that *Nevermind* allegedly prompted, and here it only is fitting to give him the last word. Interviewed separately from Krist during that same trip to Seattle shortly before the release of *In Utero* in 1993, he made it clear that Nirvana had never set out to change the industry or the world, that he didn't much care about any of that, and that the main thing that had ever mattered to him was being in a band and making music he enjoyed.

"I don't understand how these people can come from an environment and a lifestyle after so many years of being in underground music and keeping that kind of music alive, and now it suddenly seems like a desperate attempt by some of these bands who've never been recognized at trying to say we deserve that," Kurt told me. "It's kind of sickening to see how these bands become careerists all of a sudden. That's what everyone was against when they started these bands. The reason I wanted to be in a band was to be in a band and write songs. You can be validated if you sell two thousand records, and you should be happy with that."

And that is no myth.

Center: Flyer, Pukkelpop, Hasselt, Belgium, August 25, 1991. *Right:* Flyer, Aladin Music Hall, Bremen, Germany, August 27, 1991.

KURT'S TOP 50 ALBUMS

THE CLASH

Combat Rock (Epic, 1982)

The final Clash album with Mick Jones in the lineup temporarily propelled the band to early 1980s stardom. Due mostly to the Top 20 success of "Rock the Casbah," the quartet was in regular rotation on MTV and performed in front of massive audiences (e.g., Apple Computer's huge U.S. Festival in 1983). It has its moments ("Ghetto Defendant" and "Straight To Hell"), but up against such inspirational and influential classics as *London Calling*, *Give 'Em Enough Rope*, and the incendiary self-titled debut, *Combat Rock* is an odd favorite Clash album for a hungry music fanatic like Cobain. *AE*

so crisp and clean, so perfect. And that really sucks, because it sucks the soul right out of the music."

Grohl also voiced skepticism about the spiffed-up mix, but, along with Novoselic, went along with Geffen's decision to hire Wallace. The divided feelings illustrate two other vital components tied to *Nevermind*: contradiction and conflict. Cobain's dissent runs counter to his own admissions, echoed more than a year and a half earlier in multiple interviews, that Nirvana was headed in a softer, pop direction.

"We're aiming towards a poppier sound, and we've been into pop music for years," Cobain confessed to True in the March 17, 1990, issue of *Melody Maker*, back when he still spelled his name Kurdt Kobain. "It's just when we were recording *Bleach* we happened to be writing a lot of heavy songs at the time."

As can be gleaned from the Smart sessions demos, Cobain's pen and knack for arena-size hooks were pushing the band away from the beer-stained, low-budget grime that became Sub Pop's calling

THE MEAN FIDDLER PRESENTS

THE 1991 READING FESTIVAL

AUGUST BANK HOLIDAY WEEKEND

COMPERE JOHN PEEL

FRI 23rd AUGUST FROM 2PM **SAT 24th AUGUST** FROM NOON **SUN 25th AUGUST** FROM NOON

IGGY POP
SONIC YOUTH
POP WILL EAT ITSELF
DINOSAUR JNR
CHAPTERHOUSE
NIRVANA
SILVERFISH
BABES IN TOYLAND
THE HONEYTHIEVES

JAMES
CARTER THE UNSTOPPABLE SEX MACHINE
THE FALL
DE LA SOUL
BLUR
TEENAGE FANCLUB
FLOWERED UP
THE FAT LADY SINGS
KINGMAKER
MERCURY REV

THE SISTERS OF MERCY
NEDS ATOMIC DUSTBIN
THE GODFATHERS
GANG STARR
NITZER EBB
SENSELESS THINGS
KITCHENS OF DISTINCTION
SWERVEDRIVER
BONGWATER
THE FAMILY CAT

THE MEAN FIDDLER STAGE

FRIDAY - AMERICAN MUSIC CLUB · GUY CLARKE & TOWNES VAN ZANDT · SWEETMOUTH
THIN WHITE ROPE · 22 PISTEPIRKKO · INTO PARADISE · KATELL KEINEG · THE BELLTOWER · RAIN · REVOLVER
THE ROCKING BIRDS SATURDAY · EDWYN COLLINS THE MILLTON BROTHERS · FIVE THIRTY
POWER OF DREAMS · THE REAL PEOPLE · M.C.BUZZ B. · THE DYLANS · THOUSAND YARD STARE · THE SOUTHERNAIRES
THE WENDYS · THE HOLLOW MEN · BURN · WELFARE HAROINE SUNDAY · THE BLUE AEROPLANES
NEW FAST AUTOMATIC DAFFODILS · THE CROPDUSTERS · FATIMA MANSIONS · DR PHIBES AND THE HOUSE OF WAX EQUATIONS
CATHERINE WHEEL · THE POOH STICKS · CAPTAIN SENSIBLE · LOVE'S YOUNG NIGHTMARE
TOASTED HERETIC · LATE ROAD LUNATICS · THE CANDYSKINS (ARTISTS NOT IN ORDER OF APPEARANCE)

COMEDY BIG TOP

FRIDAY - DENIS LEARY · FRANK SIDEBOTTOM · MARK HIRST (MARK MIWURDZ) · TED CHIPPINGTON
DOON · RICHARD HERRING · SISTER MARY IMMACULATE · MARK LAMARR
CHRIS AND GEORGE SATURDAY · GERRY SADOWITZ · STEVE FROST (OBLIVION BOYS)
STEVE RAWLINS · BETTY SPITTLE · JAMES MACABRE · CHRIS LUBY · ALAN PARKER (URBAN WARRIOR)
BOB DILLINGER · STEWART LEE SUNDAY · SEAN HUGHES · TOMMY COCKLES · JO BRAND
DONNA McPHAIL · FELIX · OTIZ CANNELONI · WELL OILED SISTERS · MALCOM HARDEE
(ARTISTS NOT IN ORDER OF APPEARANCE)

SPECIAL 3 DAY SEASON TICKET AVAILABLE (IN ADVANCE ONLY) AT £40
(subject to booking fee) includes camping, car parking and VAT. Admissions at ground (if available) will be £18 per day
(i.e £54 for 3 days) plus camping and car parking. Tickets available at face value from The Mean Fiddler, Harlesden, NW10
Powerhaus, Islington, N.1. and Subterania, Ladbroke Grove, W10

Postal Application to: Reading Festival Dept N1, PO Box 1707, London NW10 1UX £40 (plus 50p booking fee). Enclose S.A.E. and cheque/P.O. made payable to Rockfield Promotions(Allow 28 Days For Delivery)

DON'T FORGET TO BRING A RADIO AND TUNE INTO

CREDIT CARD HOTLINES: 081 963 0940, 0272 299008, 0602 483456, 071 734 8932, 071 379
071 793 0500, 071 240 0771, 071 580 3111
INFORMATION AND COMPETITION LINE: 0836 404967 (Calls Charged at 44p Peak 33p Off P

card well before Wallace entered the fray. And for all his threats to sign to Geffen, take the money, break up, and then record for his beloved K Records under a different name, Cobain understood getting in bed with a major label offered opportunities for popularity. His reluctance toward fame ran up against strong impulses for attention.

"I don't wanna have any other kind of job, I can't work among people," the singer told Keith Cameron in an October 1990 issue of *Sounds*. "I may as well try and make a career out of this. All my life my dream has been to be a big rock star—just may as well abuse it while you can."

At other turns, drawing on his own experiences as a kid, Cobain justified Nirvana's evolution by recognizing what it could mean for a generation weaned on trite pop and Aquanet-sprayed piffle. "It'd be nice for a fifteen-year-old kid in Aberdeen to have the choice of buying a record from a band like us," he told U.K. metal rag *Kerrang!* in August 1991, several weeks before *Nevermind* hit stores. "That wasn't an opportunity I had when I was growing up. I remember reading about the Sex Pistols and the Clash in old *CREEM* magazines, and when I was finally able to find

Above: Poster, Reading Festival, Reading, Great Britain, August 23, 1991. *Middle:* Backstage pass, Reading Festival, 1991. *Right:* The "Smells Like Teen Spirit" single, also including "Drain You," "Even in His Youth," and "Aneurysm," released on September 10, 1991. *Opposite:* Cobain performing at the Reading Festival.
Doralba Picerno/S.I.N./Alamy

KURT'S TOP 50 ALBUMS

THE FAITH/VOID
The Faith/Void split LP (Dischord, 1982)
The Faith deliver solid D.C.-style hardcore on their side, but the peerless Void and their early, quite chaotic metal/hardcore crossover attack is the engine behind this split LP's inclusion in the classic canon of American hardcore releases. Anchored by the manic guitar shredding of Bubba Dupree, Void's influence on crossover legends like D.R.I., Corrosion of Conformity, and the Accused, as well as more riff-oriented heavies such as the Melvins and Black Flag's Greg Ginn, will never be up for debate. Essential. *AE*

a Clash record at the library, it was *Sandanista!* They'd already become a lame reggae band! It really turned me off punk until Black Flag came along and rescued me from my Iron Maiden records!"

Nevermind performed the same function for millions, triggering an unprecedented mushrooming of a burgeoning underground that, within a year of the album's release, became both the major labels' needed substitute for a dying rock scene and the new mainstream. Already given pole position by way of an excited indie press, industry euphoria, and its hip connection to Sub Pop, *Nevermind* received the pivotal boost that allowed it to lap the competition from the very medium that helped make unlikely megastars out of veterans like ZZ Top and Dire Straits during the 1980s.

At first glance, Nirvana's blue-collar appearance and punk-honed attitude don't seem to jive with MTV's chic identity. Yet the channel logged a history of coopting

Left: Poster *Nevermind* Tour, Fall 1991. *Middle:* Flyer, Foufounes Électriques, Montréal, Quebec, Canada, September 21, 1991. *Opposite:* Nirvana in the spotlight. *Kevin Estrada*

Nirvana plays Iguana's in Tijuana, Mexico, October 24, 1991. *Ed Sirrs/Camera Press*

fresh sounds and bold images, and turning them into safer, stylish commodities that bore illusions of subversive connotations. Such acumen peaked with the video for "Smells Like Teen Spirit," which framed communal anarchy in a professionally shot setting that nonetheless conveys subcultural mien and do-it-yourself ideals. Aptly described by Grohl as a "pep rally from hell," it looked and sounded like nothing that ever aired on MTV.

Made for $33,000, the video stands as a compromise between director Samuel Bayer and the band members, particularly Cobain, who preferred more mass destruction and mayhem. Once again, *Nevermind* reaped the benefits of being viewed through a professional filter. The video's imagery—crusty high-school gym, lonely janitor, female cheerleaders, moshing teenagers

dressed down in simple clothes, raging bonfire, fans swarming the band, tied-up teacher, and, for dramatic effect, dry-ice fog to make it appear as if the amplifiers are smoking—instantly summed up the dread, resentment, and anger associated with high-school pettiness, conformist pressure, Reagan/Bush's conservative twelve-year reign, corporate greed, and an uncertain future.

Social outcasts, artistic types, homosexuals, agitators, non-jocks, peaceniks that spoke up against the flag-waving invasion of Iraq, and individuals uninterested in canned customs such as prom, college fraternities, glee club, and cliques—they all finally had something they could call their own. The video was an extended middle finger to everyone and everything that forced them to feel bad about their choices, identities, interests, and

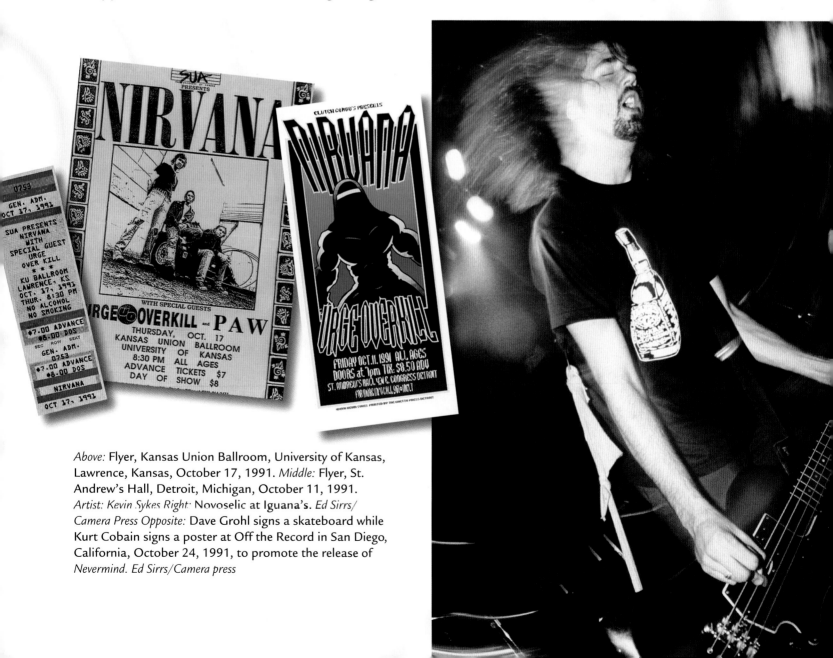

Above: Flyer, Kansas Union Ballroom, University of Kansas, Lawrence, Kansas, October 17, 1991. *Middle:* Flyer, St. Andrew's Hall, Detroit, Michigan, October 11, 1991. *Artist: Kevin Sykes Right:* Novoselic at Iguana's. *Ed Sirrs/ Camera Press Opposite:* Dave Grohl signs a skateboard while Kurt Cobain signs a poster at Off the Record in San Diego, California, October 24, 1991, to promote the release of *Nevermind. Ed Sirrs/Camera press*

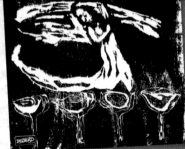

KURT'S TOP 50 ALBUMS

RITES OF SPRING

Rites of Spring (Dischord, 1985)

Terminally saddled with the "first emo band" tag (short for "emocore," itself obviously meant to imply "emotional hardcore"), Rites of Spring were formed as a reaction to the tough-guy meathead factor that had saturated hardcore by 1985. Rites of Spring were formed during D.C.'s infamous "Revolution Summer" of 1985, and played only fifteen gigs, many of which ended with members collapsed on the floor and equipment destroyed. Their sole full-length was joined by a 7-inch (also on Dischord), but a band like this was destined to be short-lived. Guitarist/vocalist Guy Picciotto and drummer Brendan Canty would go on to form the even shorter-lived Happy Go Licky before making underground-rock history as one half of Fugazi. *AE*

Nirvana performs at the Warfield Theatre, San Francisco, California, October 26, 1991. *Jay Blakesberg*

situations. Cutting through pretentiousness, phoniness, and pretense, it embodied a generation's festering boredom, stifled rage, and general malaise.

By itself, the song is an anthem. Coupled with the video, it's an invitation to a movement. Suddenly, rock seemed dangerous and capable of changing lives again. Bayer's creation gave Nirvana a relatable narrative and insightful edginess absent from Dinosaur Jr's cut-rate animated short for "The Wagon," Mudhoney's winking "Let It Slide" clip, the Pixies' artsy "Head On," and every other video circulating in MTV's *120 Minutes* rotation. Dealing with themes intimately familiar to anyone who attended high school, the "Smells Like Teen Spirit" video is anchored in a reality opposite the fantasies in the nightmarish dreamscapes in Metallica's "Enter Sandman" and psychopathic dementia of Guns N' Roses' "Don't Cry," popular period clips swollen by sky-high budgets and well-buffed sheen.

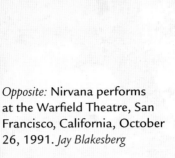

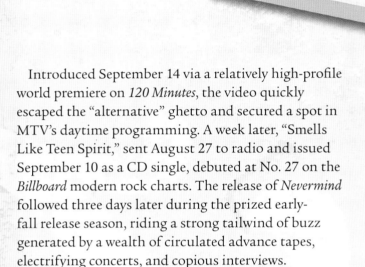

Opposite: Nirvana performs at the Warfield Theatre, San Francisco, California, October 26, 1991. *Jay Blakesberg*

Introduced September 14 via a relatively high-profile world premiere on *120 Minutes*, the video quickly escaped the "alternative" ghetto and secured a spot in MTV's daytime programming. A week later, "Smells Like Teen Spirit," sent August 27 to radio and issued September 10 as a CD single, debuted at No. 27 on the *Billboard* modern rock charts. The release of *Nevermind* followed three days later during the prized early-fall release season, riding a strong tailwind of buzz generated by a wealth of circulated advance tapes, electrifying concerts, and copious interviews.

"We did so many interviews blindly, just walking into radio stations and doing unnecessary interviews with metal magazines, anything," Cobain told Azerrad. Nirvana initiated the media blitz after informing Geffen it had been disappointed with Sub Pop's publicity efforts. While the band quickly tired of the face time with DJs and journalists, the press intensified the hype surrounding *Nevermind*. Many of the articles and radio shows appeared just before and shortly after the record's release. *Nevermind* wouldn't be a secret or surprise for anyone clued into indie channels, no matter how big or small.

Geffen shipped 46,251 copies of *Nevermind* to music retailers across the country. Stocked by regional buyers that, apart from generic empirical data, had little insight into the makeup of each location's clientele, many stores in national chains belonging to Sam Goody, Camelot, and TransWorld (Coconuts) were lucky to receive one copy on CD and another on cassette. The label's gross underestimate of public interest—mirrored by that of the domineering retailers—caused *Nevermind* to immediately sell out in most places, leaving fans

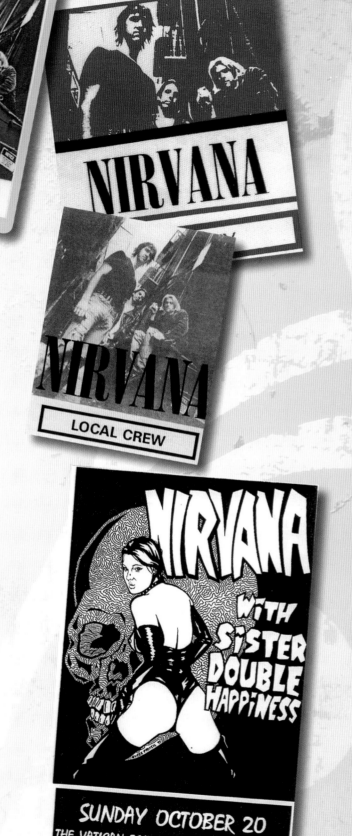

Flyer, the Vatican, Houston, Texas, October 20, 1991. *Artist: Uncle Charlie*

beat happening

Jamboree

KURT'S TOP 50 ALBUMS

BEAT HAPPENING

Jamboree (K Records, 1988)
At just under twenty-four minutes, Beat Happening's second full-length is the gold standard of American twee-pop. Vocalist and K Records founder/primary operator Calvin Johnson's baritone and the self-described "dark and sexy" vibe of this much-exalted LP is the soundtrack for an adult slumber party, and though rarely imitated, this brazen sonic trademark became extensively influential on the navel-gazing faux naïveté movement that came together immediately after *Jamboree*'s release, localizing itself around the friendly environs of Olympia's Evergreen State College. The album features the band's best-known song, "Indian Summer," described by Luna/Galaxie 500 main man Dean Warham as "indie rock's 'Knockin' on Heaven's Door' . . . everyone's done it" in the K Records documentary, *The Shield Around the K* (a reference to the label logo that Cobain had tattooed on his arm). *AE*

walking out of shops talking more about the album they couldn't attain for another few days.

While unintentional, Geffen's supply gaffe drove up demand, inflamed passions, and stimulated conversations from inner-city neighborhoods to the edges of farm towns. From a marketing perspective, the strategy smacked of genius. Without the Internet to provide instant answers and information, and only radio and MTV to turn to, new converts reveled in myths and uncertainties surrounding the band. Questions abounded.

"Who is Nirvana?" "Does the band pronounce its name 'NEAR-VAN-EER' or 'NUR-VAH-NAH'?" "Why is a naked baby on the album cover?" "Do they have other records out?" "What is he singing in that song?" "Are the lyrics available?"

Nevermind cultivated mystery, intrigue, enthusiasm, and yearning. Rather than drive people away, the obscurity of Cobain's words magnetized them in the same way the music bewitched listeners worn down by years of formula and predictability. The possible meanings of "Smells Like Teen Spirit" and identity of Nirvana became talking points around which fans bonded. The lines between the cool underground and lame mainstream evaporated. Nirvana exacerbated the latter development, but the slow fade had already commenced.

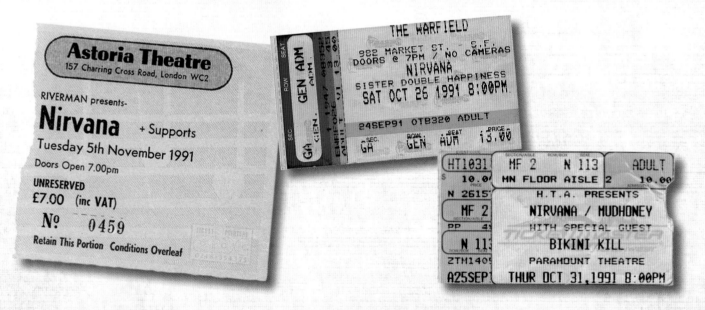

Opposite: Nirvana plays the Bierkeller, Bristol, Great Britain, November 4, 1991. *Ed Sirrs/Camera Press*

NIRVANA
MUDHONEY

MONQUI
PRESENTS

PLUS ANOTHER COOL BAND
OCTOBER 29
FOX THEATRE

TICKETS AT
GI JOE'S TICKETMASTER MUSIC MILLENNIUM

Opposite and above: Nirvana plays the Paradiso in Amsterdam, the Netherlands, November 25, 1991. *Peter Pakvis/Redferns/ Getty Images. Left:* Flyer, Fox Theatre, Portland, Oregon, October 29, 1991. *Artist: Mike King*

R.E.M.'s *Out of Time* and Jane's Addiction's *Ritual de lo Habitual*, major-label releases, scraped the glass ceiling and laid requisite groundwork in the previous months by signaling that college-rock bands could resonate with the mainstream. Neither album is as noisy, bracing, or jarring as *Nevermind*, and both rank among their respective artists' most commercial affairs. Yet they came from a world apart from that of Queensryche and Michael Jackson. Two other related factors reveal that an alternative-leaning pattern was established by the time *Nevermind* hit shelves, further validating that the album (unlike earlier, unexpected blockbusters such as Peter Frampton's *Frampton Comes*

Alive and Vanilla Ice's *To the Extreme*) didn't simply drop from the sky.

Until SoundScan materialized in March 1991, period records by the likes of Jesus & Mary Chain, Meat Puppets, Dinosaur Jr, and Sonic Youth (whose *Goo* moved 200,000 copies) undoubtedly achieved a wider reach than believed. Moreover, the ease, affordability, and prevalence of dubbing records onto cassettes for friends—a religious practice among teens and twenty-somethings—demonstrates that the underground network and audience had greatly expanded since its early-1980s genesis. Somebody was buying the indie records released by Sub Pop, Amphetamine Reptile, SST, Touch and

Cobain on stage at the Paradiso in Amsterdam, the Netherlands. *Peter Pakvis/Redferns/Getty Images*

Left: Poster, Italian Tour, Fall 1991. *Below:* Tickets, Great Britain Tour, Winter 1991.

KURT'S TOP 50 ALBUMS

TALES OF TERROR

Tales of Terror (CD Presents, 1984)
Still obscure despite the reissue treatment given America's 1980s hardcore, post-punk, proto-indie, and crossover scenes, Sacramento's Tales of Terror released only one album of their mostly unique (at the time) metallic, occasionally sludgy skate-core that sometimes has the same proto-grunge feel found on the transitional albums of Black Flag's final two years (1984–1986). *Tales of Terror* is an anomaly here in that it has never carried so much as a hint of the cultural cache or retrospective kudos that every other album on the list enjoys to at least a minor degree. *AE*

Go, Merge, Kill Rock Stars, and Matador, all of which ventured far beyond the homemade-style 7-inches issued just years earlier. And the audience was still growing.

Despite the initial shortage, *Nevermind* entered the *Billboard* charts at No. 144. It crushed expectations by contemporaneously going gold (500,000 units) and becoming the most-requested title on alternative radio by late October. AOR and hard rock stations followed by mid-November, and finally, Top 40, bowing to the inevitable, aired Nirvana before 1991 ended. By late November, *Nevermind* began shifting more than 300,000 copies per week, ultimately outperforming well-advertised releases from Jackson, U2, Brooks, and Metallica. At the end of the first week of January 1992, it topped the charts—just before the band's *Saturday Night Live* gig.

Unable to be insulated from the conflagration sparked by *Nevermind*, and on a fall tour that took the trio to small clubs overwhelmed by the ticket demand and fervent energy, Nirvana began to experience internal and external cracks that worsened over time. Its lighthearted period of ornery innocence and relative anonymity was over. The band's mid-September in-store appearance at Seattle's Beehive Records served as a harbinger of the future. More than two hundred people arrived five hours before the event started. Fans swamped the band members and asked for autographs, stunning Cobain and company in their own hometown.

"Things started to happen after that," a reflective Novoselic later told journalist Charles R. Cross, recognizing that, for better and worse, the pieces for a wholesale transformation had fallen into place. "We weren't the same old band. Kurt, he just kind of withdrew. There was a lot of personal stuff going on. It got complicated. It was more than we bargained for."

Above: Flyer, Cow Palace, Daly City, California, December 31, 1991. *Artist: Henry Rossit Below:* Cobain surfs the crowd at the Batschkapp, Frankfurt, Germany, November 12, 1991. *Peter Pakvis/Redferns/Getty Images*

KURT'S TOP 50 ALBUMS

Above: Band portrait in Frankfurt, Germany, November 12, 1991. *Peter Pakvis/Redferns/Getty Images. Below:* Poster, Australian Tour, Winter 1992. *Artist: Ben Brown*

LEADBELLY
Leadbelly's Last Sessions, Vol. 1
(Smithsonian Folkways, 1994)
A four-CD set of the legendary country blues guitarist's 1948 sessions and his only commercial recordings. Committed to tape at the tail end of his employment (as a guide and driver) by blues and folk historian and archivist John Lomax, Leadbelly would succumb to Lou Gehrig's disease in 1953. A man who sung his way out of prison after killing another man over a woman (one of two homicides he served time for), Leadbelly had far-reaching influence in the realms of 1970s hard/blues-rock and early-1960s activist folk music of the type preferred by Bob Dylan in his early career. *AE*

A MAGNET PROMOTION

Magnet Proms. & Triple J
present **NIRVANA**
+ MEANIES + TUMBLEWEED

THEBARTON THEATRE

THURSDAY JANUARY 30 1992
Tickets: $20+b/f

0422

FRI JAN 24 · PHOENECIAN CLUB · SYDNEY
SAT JAN 25 · BIG DAY OUT FESTIVAL · SYDNEY
SUN JAN 26 · FISHERMAN'S WARF · GOLD COAST
MON JAN 27 · BRISBANE FESTIVAL HALL · BRISBANE
WED JAN 29 · METROPOLIS · PERTH
THURS JAN 30 · THE OLD LION · ADELAIDE
FRI JAN 31 · THE PALACE · MELBOURNE
SAT FEB 1 · THE PALACE (ALL AGE SHOW) · MELBOURNE
WED FEB 5 · ANU BAR · CANBERRA

PRESENTED NATIONALLY BY TRIPLE J
TICKETS AVAILABLE AT USUAL OUTLETS

Cobain plays the Astoria, London, 1991. *Denis O'Regan/ Getty Images*

Initially, Nirvana's overwhelmed feelings translated into the band's disdainful attitude toward the media. Cobain, who in his journals confessed to have delved into heroin before the release of *Nevermind*, allegedly to ease perpetual stomach pain, began seeing how many lies he could tell to journalists and DJs. He soon ceded most press duties to Novoselic and Grohl, who begrudgingly kept a more even-keeled attitude. Cobain's indie elitism paralleled his contradictory personality. The same singer who had bellyached about the state of popular music and lamented that fans were kept in the dark by major labels reversed course as *Nevermind* exploded, dismissing new fans as inferior and unwelcome.

"I found myself being overly obnoxious during the *Nevermind* tour because I noticed that there were more average people coming into our shows and I didn't want them there," he told Azerrad. "They started to get on my nerves. I was obnoxious and showing my weenie and acting like a freak and dancing around and wearing dresses and just being drunk. I would say things like 'All right! Frat rock! Look at all these frat rock geeks out here!'"

Intended as ironic and humorous, the insults come across as jejune remarks pulled by an artist torn by his own polarizing desires—the living embodiment of the chorus to "In Bloom," a song cradled by a supremely catchy pop hook in non-ironic fashion. Rather than turn fame into a positive like Perry Farrell, who founded a festival that realized the objectives of placing attention on deserving artists and subcultural affairs, Cobain became guilty of the same pretentious mentality and self-indulgence he supposedly despised. Similarly, the group's destruction of instruments, amplifiers, and hotel rooms quickly devolved into a routine as predictably cliché as pyrotechnics at a Bon Jovi concert. Cobain's explanation for the mayhem—a reaction against being

KURT'S TOP 50 ALBUMS

MUDHONEY
Superfuzz Bigmuff (Sub Pop, 1988)
The 1988 EP by Mudhoney is one of the more exciting, timeless, and influential releases to come out of the Seattle underground immediately preceding the industry-altering grunge explosion. Merging the Stooges, Black Flag, early Melvins, and garage-rock, the extremely loud six-song *Superfuzz Bigmuff* is named after the Univox Super-Fuzz and Electro-Harmonix Big Muff guitar effects that the band favored at the time. Combined with the surprise indie success of Mudhoney's debut single, "Touch Me, I'm Sick," released just two months prior, *Superfuzz Bigmuff* helped to establish Mudhoney as Sub Pop's flagship band. *AE*

Left: The *Hormoaning* EP was released in January 1992 in Australia and Japan only to promote Nirvana Pacific Rim Tour. This is the Australian cover. *Below:* The Japanese edition of *Hormoaning*. The EP was re-released in the United States for Record Store Day 2011 as a limited edition.

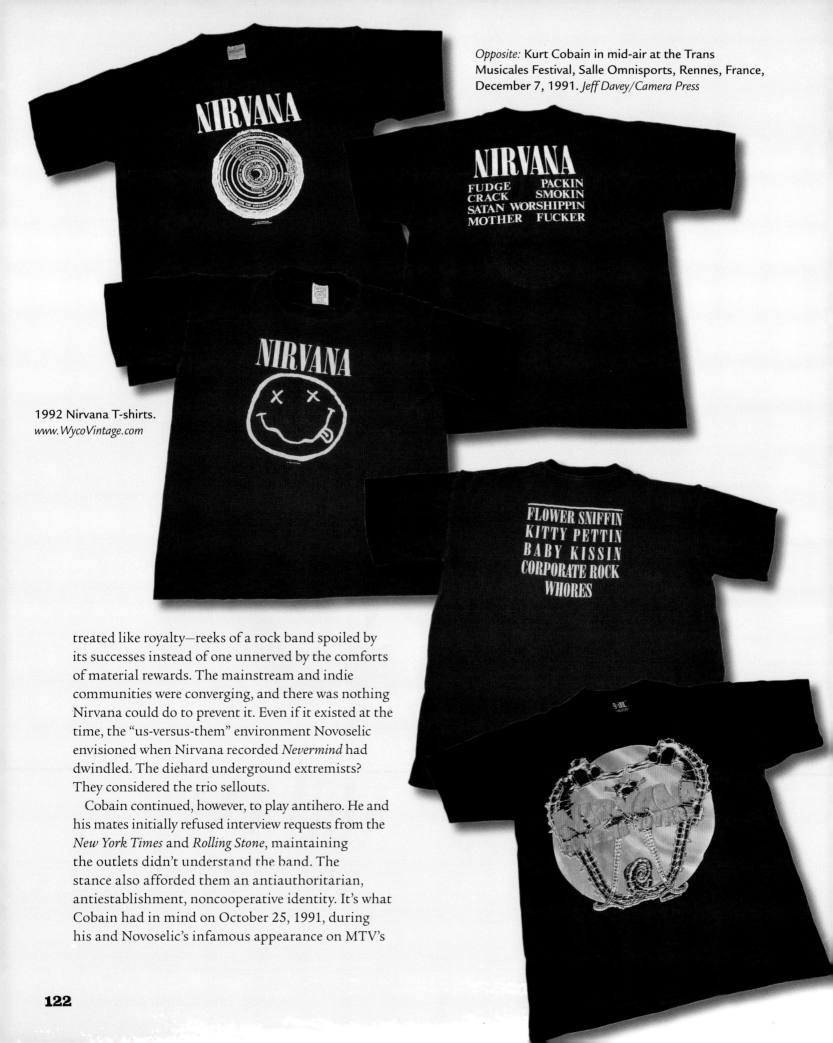

NIRVANA

NIRVANA
FUDGE   PACKIN
CRACK   SMOKIN
SATAN WORSHIPPIN
MOTHER   FUCKER

Opposite: Kurt Cobain in mid-air at the Trans Musicales Festival, Salle Omnisports, Rennes, France, December 7, 1991. *Jeff Davey/Camera Press*

NIRVANA

1992 Nirvana T-shirts.
www.WycoVintage.com

FLOWER SNIFFIN
KITTY PETTIN
BABY KISSIN
CORPORATE ROCK
WHORES

treated like royalty—reeks of a rock band spoiled by its successes instead of one unnerved by the comforts of material rewards. The mainstream and indie communities were converging, and there was nothing Nirvana could do to prevent it. Even if it existed at the time, the "us-versus-them" environment Novoselic envisioned when Nirvana recorded *Nevermind* had dwindled. The diehard underground extremists? They considered the trio sellouts.

Cobain continued, however, to play antihero. He and his mates initially refused interview requests from the *New York Times* and *Rolling Stone*, maintaining the outlets didn't understand the band. The stance also afforded them an antiauthoritarian, antiestablishment, noncooperative identity. It's what Cobain had in mind on October 25, 1991, during his and Novoselic's infamous appearance on MTV's

Right: Novoselic performs at a secret Nirvana gig at the Carver Gymnasium, Western Washington University, Bellingham, Washington, October 2, 1992. *Charles Peterson/ Retna Ltd./Corbis*
Opposite: Grohl plays the Crocodile Cafe, Seattle, Washington, October 4, 1992. *Charles Peterson/ Retna Ltd./Corbis*
Below: Nirvana's "Come As You Are" single, also featuring "Endless, Nameless," "School" (live), and "Drain You" (live), released on March 3, 1992.

NIRVANA

come as you are

KURT'S TOP 50 ALBUMS

DANIEL JOHNSTON

Yip/Jump Music (Stress Music/Homestead, 1983/1989)

When British music critic Everett True gave Cobain a Daniel Johnston "Hi, How Are You?" T-shirt, little did he know that Cobain's affinity for the garment would shoot already burgeoning interest in the Texas outsider indie-busker through the roof and create a major-label bidding war while Johnston was hospitalized for his worsening mental state. The T-shirt is now an iconic piece of Cobain-wear, but it was Johnston's fifth self-released cassette, *Yip/Jump Music* (or probably Homestead Records' 1989 proper CD and vinyl reissue) that Cobain held in higher regard, leading to yet another example of the Nirvana man's magical music-world philanthropy. *AE*

Above: Poster, le Zénith, Paris, France, June 24, 1992.
Right: Poster, Sjöhistoriska Museet, Stockholm, Sweden, June 30, 1992.

Headbanger's Ball. The weekly show hailed music whose machismo, misogyny, materialism, posturing, and glamour the band detested.

Outfitted in a hideous yellow gown and hiding behind sunglasses, Cobain acts like a bratty eleven-year-old dragged to a social function by his parents, the kid who would rather be playing with friends and, since he didn't get his way, revolts by making everyone else's lives miserable until he gets to leave. During a one-sided conversation with host Riki Rachtman, he says almost nothing, mumbles two-word replies, and looks both lifeless and joyless. Cobain's behavior makes a resistive statement and throws down the gauntlet at metal fans. Yet his saturnine disposition extinguishes any potential for wit, which would have made him appear smarter and sharper. Had someone like Mudhoney's Mark Arm or the Pixies' Frank Black been in Cobain's chair, it's impossible to imagine either missing the chance to crack wise and have fun.

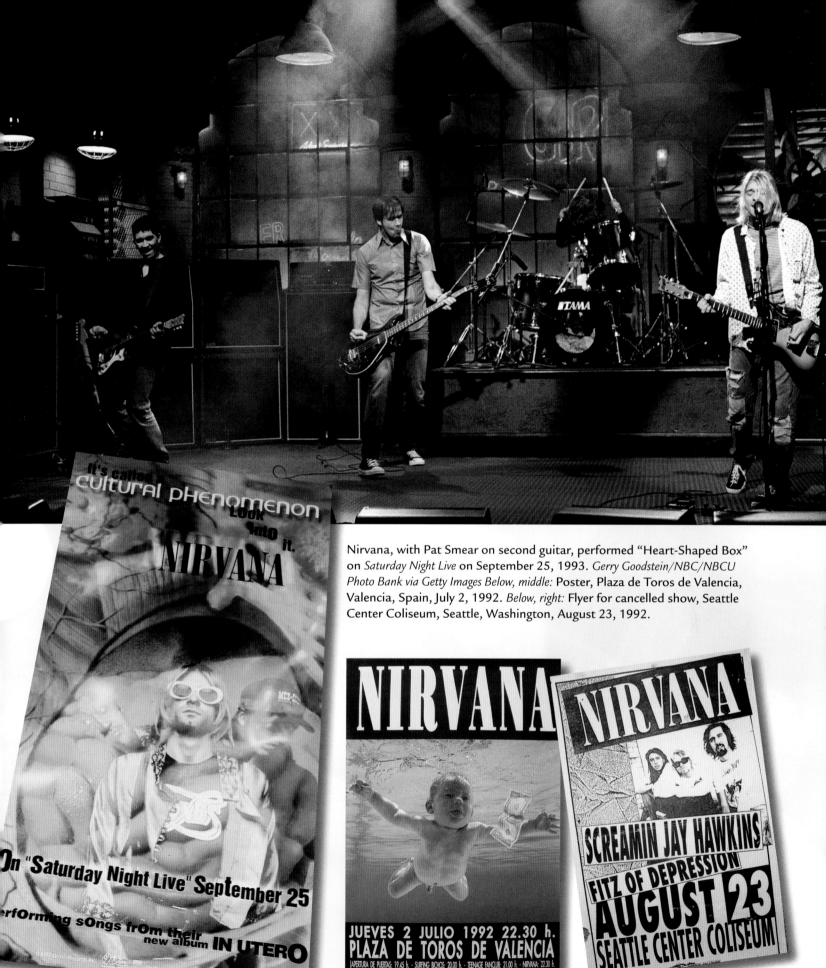

Nirvana, with Pat Smear on second guitar, performed "Heart-Shaped Box" on *Saturday Night Live* on September 25, 1993. *Gerry Goodstein/NBC/NBCU Photo Bank via Getty Images Below, middle:* Poster, Plaza de Toros de Valencia, Valencia, Spain, July 2, 1992. *Below, right:* Flyer for cancelled show, Seattle Center Coliseum, Seattle, Washington, August 23, 1992.

it's called
CULTURAL PHENOMENON
LOOK into it.

NIRVANA

On "Saturday Night Live" September 25

erfOrming sOngs frOm their
new album IN UTERO

NIRVANA

JUEVES 2 JULIO 1992 22.30 h.
PLAZA DE TOROS DE VALENCIA

(APERTURA DE PUERTAS: 19.45 h. · SURFING BICHOS: 20.00 h. · TEENAGE FANCLUB: 21.00 h. · NIRVANA: 22.30 h.
VENTA ANTICIPADA: 3.000 PTAS. VENTA ANTICIPADA EN PUNTOS HABITUALES

NIRVANA

SCREAMIN JAY HAWKINS
FITZ OF DEPRESSION
AUGUST 23
SEATTLE CENTER COLISEUM

Rolling Stone's April 1992 Nirvana cover story brought out Cobain's lighter side. He sported a home-made "Corporate Magazines Still Suck" T-shirt for the photo shoot, eschewing the magazine's plans to dress up the members in Brooks Brothers suits. "Kurt was very resistant," said photographer Mark Seliger. "He didn't want to be publicized. He didn't want anything but to be true to his fans and to the music."

Of course, Cobain alone chose to be publicized. He could have abstained from the public eye. In spite of his protestations to the contrary, the singer seemingly craved attention. His made-for-reality-TV relationship with Courtney Love, in full bloom by early 1992,

made matters worse. Their soap-opera romance, drug habits, wedding, and baby soon overshadowed Nirvana. Cobain may have been anointed the spokesperson of his generation, but his health problems led to Nirvana scrapping scores of dates between December 1991 and the following fall.

"From nobodies to superstars to fuck-ups in the space of six months! That had to be a record," wrote Keith Cameron in an unflattering August 29, 1992

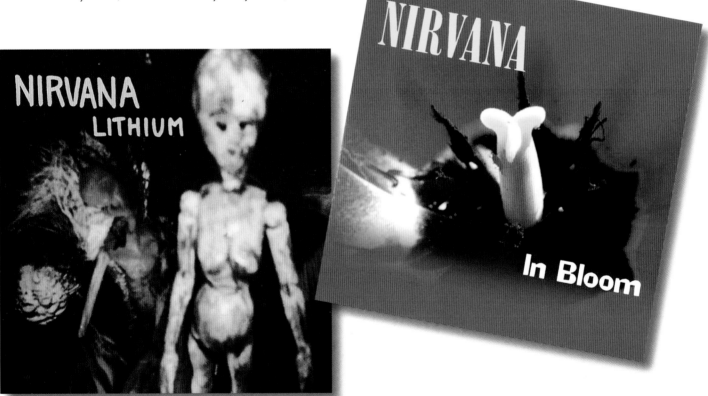

Left: Nirvana's "Lithium" single, also featuring "Been A Son" (live), "Curmudgeon," and "D-7," released on July 21, 1992.
Right: Nirvana's "In Bloom" single, also featuring "Sliver" (live) and "Polly" (live), released on November 30, 1992.

IN A SPECIAL PERFORMANCE
TO HEIMEFTT THE NO 9 CAMPAIGN

IN CONCERT ★ ★ ★ ★ ★ HONOUI PRESENTS ★ ★ ★ ★ ★ OUTDOORS

NIRVANA
HELMET
POISON IDEA
CALAMITY JANE
+
EMCEE • JELLO BIAFRA

THURS. SEPT. 10

PORTLAND MEADOWS

FOOD BOOTHS • BEER & WINE GARDEN

Above: Nirvana at Pier 28 in Seattle, Washington, December 13, 1993, for the taping of the *MTV Live and Loud: Nirvana Performs Live* television special. *Jeff Kravitz/FilmMagic/Getty Images*
Left: Flyer, Portland Meadows, Portland, Oregon, September 10, 1992.

Left: Nirvana's compilation album, *Incesticide*, released on December 12, 1992.
Right: Nirvana's "Heart-Shaped Box" single, also featuring "Milk It" and "Marigold," released on August 23, 1993.
Below: Following wounds won from his exuberant performance on *MTV Live and Loud*, Krist Novoselic gets his hand patched up by firefighter paramedics backstage. *Jeff Kravitz/FilmMagic/ Getty Images*

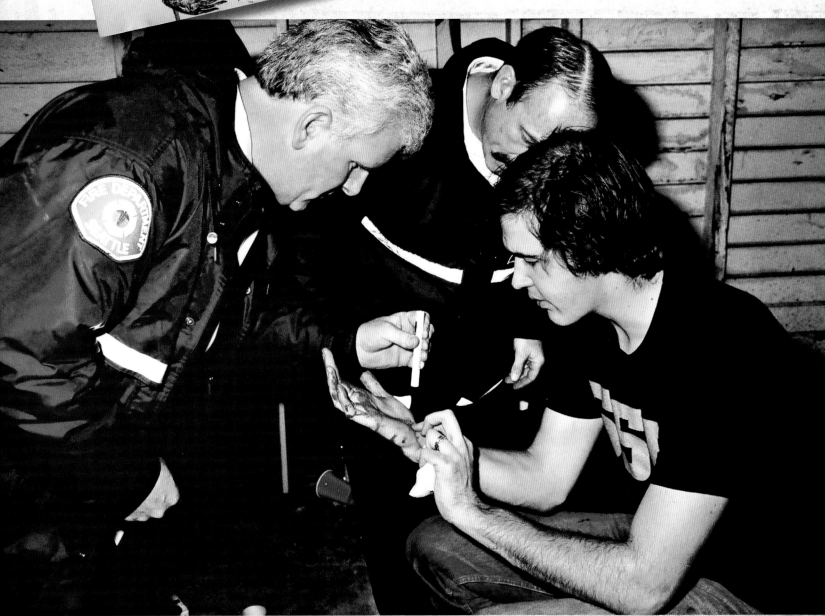

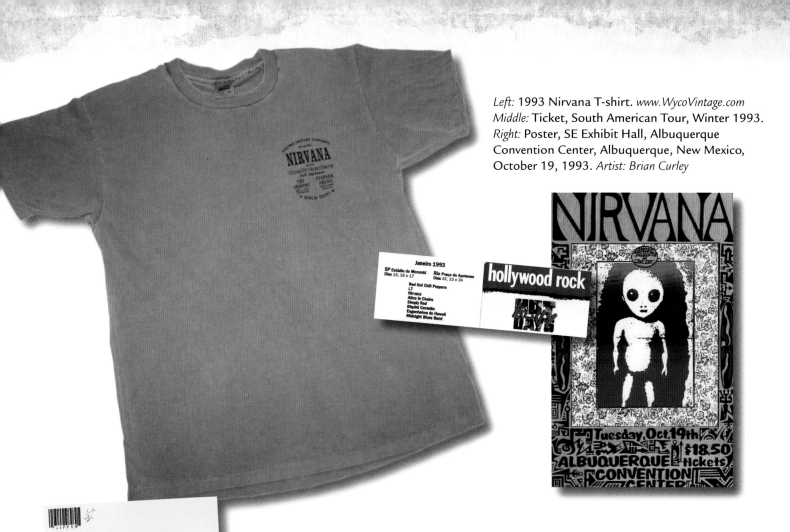

Left: 1993 Nirvana T-shirt. *www.WycoVintage.com*
Middle: Ticket, South American Tour, Winter 1993.
Right: Poster, SE Exhibit Hall, Albuquerque
Convention Center, Albuquerque, New Mexico,
October 19, 1993. *Artist: Brian Curley*

ALBUM

GENERIC FLIPPER

KURT'S TOP 50 ALBUMS

FLIPPER

Generic Flipper (Subterranean, 1982)
Flipper's heavy, ultra-slow tempos and equal-opportunity "don't give a f***" audience/fan antagonism was peerless in the context of American hardcore/post-punk during the scene's 1981–1983 heyday. Primarily conceived as a way to torture and infuriate hardcore audiences, Flipper was actually popular (begrudgingly so) relative to their chosen scene, and is largely responsible for the next several years of hardcore bands that slowed down and got heavy, like Black Flag, Melvins, Butthole Surfers, Fang, and NYC's Hose (the brainchild of unknown NYU student Rick Rubin). *AE*

New Music Express story, harshly, albeit bluntly, summarizing Nirvana's rollercoaster year after he interviewed the members in July. The piece coincided with the trio's appearance at England's Reading Festival, at which a smock-adorned Cobain is rolled out in a wheelchair (pushed by a British music journalist, Everett True) in a visual display intended to ridicule what he perceived as a sensationalist press and its associated speculation of his drug abuse and fragile emotional state. Nirvana proceeded to play a show regarded by many fans as its finest performance. Punctuated by an early version of "All Apologies" and, fittingly, a lacerating cover of Fang's sardonic "The Money Will Roll Right In," it both stands as one of the group's few 1992 highlights and caps the tumultuous twelve-month period that elapsed since the release of *Nevermind.*

While the album altered the band's dynamic, outlook, and wellness in manners more negative than positive, it achieved Nirvana's goals by bringing wider recognition—and more money—to people and groups

Left: Family portrait: Courtney Love and Kurt Cobain with their daughter, Frances Bean Cobain. *Jeff Kravitz/FilmMagic/Getty Images* *Opposite:* Alone on stage. *Archives du 7eme Art/Photos 12/Alamy*

Left: Nirvana's "All Apologies" single, released in December 1993. *Right:* An *In Utero* T-Shirt

Nirvana admired, such as Mudhoney and the Melvins, which scored deals with the majors after the Great Grunge Rush commenced in spring 1992. Having received a 2 percent royalty on each copy of *Nevermind* sold, Sub Pop went from a bankrupt label that couldn't afford to pay its bands to an in-the-black tastemaker whose roster turned into a feeding trough for major labels. With its black-and-white square logo appearing on every *Nevermind* CD, tape, and LP produced, Sub Pop became a stamp of credibility and carrier of cool that hadn't been seen in the industry since Blue Note's jazz heyday in the late 1950s and early 1960s.

The financial windfall also allowed the imprint to invest in a newer crop of artists that hailed from outside the Pacific Northwest. Red Red Meat, Supersuckers,

Spinanes, Codeine, and Sebadoh all released highly respected records that existed apart from the hyped commercial "alt-rock" realm—a field that by 1993 was already becoming diluted with homogenous sounds, store-bought looks, and faux aggression.

Ironically, Cobain's friends and former label enjoyed the fruits of *Nevermind* more than its primary architect. He glibly deemed the working title of Nirvana's next album *I Hate Myself and Want to Die*, a name intended—just like his flippant wheelchair entrance at Reading—to shock and mock those who thought he wallowed in depression and junk. On the surface, it was a clever and humorous defense, equally droll and self-disparaging. But, in short time, the facetious façade would give way to a tragic truth.

A Fender Stratocaster smashed by Kurt Cobain during the 1993 tours. *Tina Paul/Camera Press*

4.

I GOT A NEW COMPLAINT
THE *IN UTERO* YEARS

By Todd Martens

Kurt Cobain photographed in his pajamas at
the Four Seasons Hotel, Seattle, Washington.
Charles Peterson/Retna Ltd./Corbis

Fifteen years after the death of Kurt Cobain, it was as if those who were once closest to him had seen something more frightening than a ghost of the fallen rock icon. Footage of Cobain—images that few had ever seen before—were spreading throughout the Internet.

The videos captured a digital representation of Cobain, complete with tattered jeans and scruffy blonde hair. He teetered around the microphone stand, a little bit wobbly and clearly in need of the backbone support that can be provided by rock 'n' roll. It was a rather impressive, albeit pixilated, re-creation. The only problem was the music.

It wasn't Nirvana staples such as "Sliver" or "Smells Like Teen Spirit" that the videos showed. It was Bon Jovi's "You Give Love a Bad Name." This, to those who grew up with Nirvana and lived with Cobain, was sacrilegious. It was also the bread and butter of *Guitar Hero*, one of the biggest video game franchises of the 2000s.

Most artists weren't averse to the game. Hard rock bands such as Metallica and Van Halen even leant their brands to *Guitar Hero*, which allowed gamers to use toy guitars to play along with digital avatars that appropriated their favorite rock stars, whether they were dead or alive or had any say in the matter. Cobain, it was quickly reasoned, would have hated it. And the Nirvana camp—a decade and a half after the sudden dissolution of the band—found itself in a familiar position: on offense.

Backstage passes, *In Utero* Tour, 1993–1994.

KURT'S TOP 50 ALBUMS

THE BEATLES
Meet The Beatles! (Capitol, 1964)
The Beatles' second album (despite a tagline on the cover that claimed it to be the first) appealed to Cobain's much-mused-upon pop tendencies and love of the Beatles (John Lennon in particular) and featured "I Want to Hold Your Hand" and "I Saw Her Standing There." Reportedly, Cobain wrote "About a Girl" from Bleach after a long listening jag with this album. *AE*

Poster, Hara Arena, Dayton, Ohio, October 30, 1993. *Artist: Lee Bolton*

Surviving members Dave Grohl and Krist Novoselic released a joint statement saying they were "dismayed and very disappointed" by the portrayal of Cobain in the game. Widow Courtney Love, who *Guitar Hero* maker Activision said had signed off on the usage of Cobain, slammed the ability to use Cobain to perform non-Nirvana songs as "disgusting."

Nirvana was no more, but the 2009 *Guitar Hero* drama essentially picked up where Cobain had left the band on April 5, 1994. His death by suicide followed nearly a year and a half of constant drama, as the period before and after the release of Nirvana's final studio album, *In Utero*, placed the band in the role of cultural warriors. *In Utero* would ultimately become the alt-rock-era's most defining moment and, in hindsight, the beginning of its end.

By the time Nirvana was starting to think about its follow-up to *Nevermind*, the outcasts, the misfits, and the ironically unkempt rockers were not only cool, they were in demand. The question this raised—have I become what I hate?—was the heart of the existential crisis of the alt-rock era, and one Nirvana

obsessed over, at least publically. Cobain and Love spent much of 1992 and 1993 in Los Angeles, and Cobain in 1992 told British publication *New Musical Express* what it was like to listen to college radio in Southern California.

"They were playing a lot of my favorite bands, like Flipper and the Melvins," Cobain said. "I was saying to myself, 'This is great.' And then the DJ came on and went on this half-hour rant about how Nirvana is so obviously business oriented and just because we have colored hair doesn't mean we are alternative. And I felt really terrible. Because there is nothing in the world I like more than pure underground music, and to be shunned by this claim that just because you are playing the corporate game you are not honest? You use the corporate ogre to your advantage. You fight them by joining them."

And fight Nirvana did. There were battles with their label, Geffen, with *In Utero* producer Steve Albini, with the press, with MTV, and with their own image. There were battles among band members, and, of course, there were battles between Love and Cobain.

Nirvana on tour.
Pictorial Press Ltd/Alamy

IN UTERO

by Greg Kot

In the summer of 1991, shortly before it became apparent that Nirvana's second album, *Nevermind*, would do for punk and the sale of flannel shirts what the Beatles on Ed Sullivan did for the British Invasion, Kurt Cobain was already expressing misgivings about how the "pros" had compromised his band's major-label debut.

"I don't think it really sounds like us," he said. He had enjoyed working with Butch Vig, who produced the album, but the mix by Andy Wallace felt cold and very un-punk rock to him. Never mind (ahem) that Wallace's gleaming mix (the guy was good enough for Slayer, after all) was in many ways the bridge between Cobain's hooky but noisy songs and the play lists of commercial radio programmers.

The singer wanted success, and lots of it, but on his terms. Dave Grohl recalled a meeting in the office of Columbia Records boss Don Ienner when Nirvana was shopping for a label. "So what do you want?" Ienner asked. "We want to be the biggest band in the world," Cobain responded. Grohl nearly fell out of his chair; it was shocking to hear a little indie band from the Pacific Northwest talking about global supremacy. For ten years, Grohl had grown up in a subterranean community whose members instinctively knew they were not welcome in Don Ienner's world—nor did the punks even want to be a part of it.

But Cobain had grand designs; he aimed to bum-rush the charts with the type of music perfected by one of his favorite '80s labels, Chicago-based Touch and Go. In the late '80s, the singer had sent a demo to Touch and Go's Corey Rusk in hope of securing a deal and was rejected. Rusk, in later years, acknowledged that his usually impeccable ears let one get away. But Cobain never lost his obsession with Touch and Go and the Chicago noise-punk aesthetic as epitomized by such bands as Big Black and the Jesus Lizard. The first three or four times I interviewed Cobain in the late '80s and early '90s, he solicited information about Big Black's former singer and guitarist, Steve Albini, whose Chicago recording studio had become a magnet for low-budget bands looking to record no-nonsense, in-your-face punk records.

In the spring of 1992, Nirvana cut a split single with the Jesus Lizard (the limited-edition single was eventually released in early 1993 and quickly sold out). Even after selling millions of copies of *Nevermind*, Cobain was eager to maintain a connection to the world of basement concerts and punk-rock 7-inch singles that had nurtured him in the '80s. Cobain was talking about having Albini produce Nirvana's third studio album as early as 1991, and when it came time to record *In Utero*, Albini got the job.

A two-week February 1993 recording session on neutral ground—snowbound Pachyderm Studio in Cannon Falls, Minnesota—left Cobain and band mates Krist Novoselic and Dave Grohl buzzing. "They were ecstatic," Albini reported a few weeks later. The engineer, who had misgivings about the band's originality—or lack thereof—before he met them was impressed with the quality of their songs and their willingness to blow them up.

For Cobain, the sessions were a rush: at last, he had gotten to make the Touch and Go record of his dreams on a major label's dime. The opening "Serve the Servants" gets gut-punch ugly, with Cobain's voice wobbling like a guitar being detuned in the middle of a chord. "Tourette's" and "Scentless Apprentice" are Jesus Lizard tracks in everything but name, with Cobain at times squealing like he's being garroted. Grohl's sticks land like bricks on the drums—a harsh thud that mocks the artificial snare shots heard on most mainstream rock productions.

"Rape Me" is closer in spirit to the addictive hookiness of *Nevermind*, with an opening riff that echoes "Smells Like Teen Spirit." The connection to Nirvana's biggest hit is purely intentional, particularly when Cobain screams, "Rape me!" some twenty times. He compresses into eleven lines of verse the then-current crisis in Bosnia-Herzegovina, where tens of thousands of women had been raped by Serbian soldiers; a reference to "Polly," an earlier Nirvana song about sexual violence; and his own rancor about being turned into a media "celebrity."

Yet all was not unrelenting chaos. Cobain's songs had moved from teen angst fueled by anger and sarcasm to deeper reservoirs of anxiety and disconnection. *In Utero* was far bolder than the somewhat streamlined, pop-focused *Nevermind* because it was not only nastier and messier, but also more vulnerable and exposed, particularly on the cello-enhanced power-pop of "All Apologies" and the bittersweet Vaselines-like "Dumb."

The range of the record was in keeping with Albini's natural room-sound aesthetic. Rather than compressing the sounds toward a middle ground compatible with radio airplay, he mixed the album to dramatize its loud-quiet dynamics. "It sounds different than any record made this year," the recording engineer claimed soon after the sessions. "It's not a record for wimps."

The decision-makers at the band's Geffen label were not nearly so impressed. One exec told me soon after the sessions that the label considered the Albini recording "unreleasable." Officially, a Geffen publicist would only confirm that the original July 1993 release date for the album had been pushed back indefinitely because of a "hang-up with mixing and mastering."

Albini had been on the phone with Cobain, who was no longer "ecstatic" about the record but "confused and distressed." "Every person they work for tells them it's terrible," said the producer, who predicted that the Pachyderm version of *In Utero* would never be released without an extensive overhaul. My reporting in the *Chicago Tribune* on Albini's comments, Geffen's foot-dragging, and Cobain's dilemma was picked up by other publications, and the Nirvana camp circled the wagons. Cobain lashed out. After he and his wife, Courtney Love, had been worked over in the celebrity media in 1992, he was in no mood to have his struggles with his record company put under a journalistic microscope. He canceled an interview he had scheduled with me that summer and then tried to ban me from covering a Nirvana concert in Chicago in November.

In retrospect, the machinations surrounding *In Utero* were not unlike those surrounding countless other major-label releases with multiplatinum sales expectations. Cobain wanted to keep up appearances. His punk-rock credibility was under attack, but he also wanted a record that wouldn't be a complete turnoff to the bigger audience he craved. Eventually, he would have R.E.M. producer Scott Litt remix a couple of tracks to boost their pop spiffiness. Albini criticized the mastering for robbing the recording of some of its punch and range. But most fans, ultimately, didn't care. The album sold millions anyway.

Journals, Cobain's posthumously issued book of personal writings, revealed that he entertained the idea of a marketing campaign for *In Utero* in which he would release two versions of the album: one called *I Hate Myself and Want to Die*, consisting of the more radical "punk rock" Albini mix, and another called *Verse Chorus Verse* that would be the "radio friendly, unit-shifting, compromise version." That sort of conflict made Cobain run; he had a clear vision of what he wanted, but the politics of getting there made him feel guilty and hypocritical.

With *In Utero*, Nirvana had made another best-selling album, but that was never the whole point, either. Punk had taught a generation to be suspicious of rock stars, and now Cobain found himself one of the biggest rock stars on the planet. To him, something about this still didn't feel right. Not for nothing does the first line on *In Utero* declare, "Teenage angst has paid off well."

Postscript: I reviewed the first of two Nirvana concerts at the Aragon Ballroom in Chicago in November 1993. Cobain was still upset about the Albini article and called the next day. "How'd you get in?" were his first words. But after a few minutes, he was chatting about the show and the songs on *In Utero*. The old Kurt was back, happy to be talking music. Finally, he asked, "Is Albini pissed at me?"

In Utero was released by David Geffen Company on September 21, 1993.

KURT'S TOP 50 ALBUMS

HALF JAPANESE
We Are They Who Ache with Amorous Love
(TEC Tones, 1990)
The eighth album by David and Jad Fair's minimal, proto-lo-fi endeavor was recorded after David became a temporary member and the lineup expanded to a somewhat stable four-piece that included Moe Tucker's sideman, John Sluggett. Tucker herself would produce Half Japanese's next album, the UFO-themed *Fire in the Sky* (1992). The duo, formed in 1975 and responsible for a sprawling and unbelievably raw triple-LP box set (*Half-Gentleman/Not Beasts*), continues to exact a huge impact on underground rock. *AE*

A lot has happened in the years since the end of Nirvana. The Millennials who followed Generation X could even be forgiven for wondering what all the *Guitar Hero* fuss was about, forgetting that the gap between Nirvana and Bon Jovi wasn't just one of personal taste and musicianship. Nirvana had once positioned itself as a band on the front lines of all things underground, even, at times, dismissing the slick production of *Nevermind*.

What's more, well into 1992 and 1993, long after *Nevermind* had conquered rock radio, Nirvana members were still defending their decision to sign with a major label. Their wealth and whether they were sellouts were constant storylines. At times, the band members found themselves trying to articulate what distinguished Nirvana from the other alt-rock bands of the era. Cobain, for instance, was never shy about his disdain of fellow Seattle-ites Pearl Jam, and Novoselic had a rant or two in him as well.

Cobain summarized the cultural battle lines to the *NME*. "You can either be a moody visionary like Michael Stipe," he said, referring to the lead singer of R.E.M., "or a mindless heavy metal party guy like Sammy Hagar."

Cobain was exaggerating for sarcastic effect, but it's no secret which side of such a spectrum he saw himself on. The subtext in Cobain's phrasing was this: There are those who play music to party, and those who play music because there is no other option.

Twenty years later, Nirvana's war is long over. A once-underground punk band like Green Day has had a hit on Broadway, and rock acts are no longer chided for lending their songs to commercials and TV shows but celebrated for it. In the 2000s, it became news when a band didn't license its music to a product, as orchestral indie act Arcade Fire found out when it rejected advances from NBC in 2007.

And Novoselic, who once took a shot at "Jessie's Girl" composer Rick Springfield in *Request* magazine, was no longer associating his personal likes and dislikes with his public image. In fact, in early 2013 Novoselic and Grohl were jamming with Springfield at a Los Angeles concert to celebrate the release of Grohl's documentary on the famed recording facility Sound City.

So when Grohl and Novoselic took up arms against *Guitar Hero*, they did so as if it was still 1994. It was the only clear option—their former bandleader didn't live to see the day when the underground and the commercial could exist and profit in perfect harmony. It was, perhaps, even Cobain's death that made it clear to independent artists that there was another option than existing to fight the corporate ogre.

Nirvana's *In Utero* was released on September 13, 1993, but the band's *In Utero* era unofficially began on September 9, 1992. The latter was the date of the annual MTV Video Music Awards, and the band's appearance was a victory lap for the trio. *Nevermind* had topped the charts way back at the start of 1992 and the band was winding down the promotional cycle for their major label debut.

What happened instead was a moment that crystallized Nirvana's appeal and cemented the band's persona as one of rebelliously bratty pop-culture party crashers. It's important to note that as big as Nirvana had become, the band and its grunge brethren comprised just a fraction of the pop landscape. Guns N' Roses' heavy metal opus, *Use Your Illusion I*, released a couple weeks prior to *Nevermind*, was still a Top 20 album on the *Billboard* charts at the time of the MTV awards while *Nevermind* was not. Lighthearted

country singer Billy Ray Cyrus had the No. 1 album in September 1992, vocal acrobat Mariah Carey was inescapable, and TLC was ushering in a new wave of female-assertive R&B. Nirvana had not permanently changed the pop landscape—not yet, anyway. But the band was about to prove once and for all that if the business of pop couldn't be completely overthrown, it could very much be infiltrated.

At the MTV awards, Nirvana had intended to perform "Rape Me," a song that had popped up in Nirvana live shows and would ultimately become a centerpiece of *In Utero*. It's a scrappy little response to "Smells Like Teen Spirit," echoing its guitar riff but sounding more like a distress call than a call to arms. There are political and social implications in what Cobain is yelping, at least for those willing to look past the title and the hollered chorus.

"It's like she's saying, 'Rape me, go ahead, rape me, beat me. You'll never kill me. I'll survive this and I'm gonna fucking rape you one of these days and you won't even know it'," Cobain told *Spin* in late 1993, describing the song then as an aural message of strength and defiance.

Poster, New York Coliseum, New York City, November 14, 1993.

Nirvana tapes the *MTV Unplugged* special at Sony Studios, New York City, November 18, 1993. *Frank Micelotta/Getty Images*

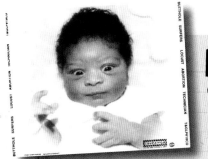

MTV producers clearly heard it differently. Though even the song's critics would agree that it's more lyrically complex than its shock-inducing title—is it a comment on misogyny or simply a look at the band's treatment in the media?—the network, as documented in Charles R. Cross' Cobain biography, *Heavier Than Heaven*, threatened to cut to commercial if Nirvana played the song.

Cobain, who was taking a break from rehab to appear at the awards, later spoke of being pressured into performing on the telecast. Soon after the MTV awards, Cobain and Love told British publication *Melody Maker* that MTV had threatened to stop playing Nirvana, as well as acts represented by Nirvana's management, if the group declined to perform. It wasn't, in short, the kind of promotional opportunity bands turned down.

Yet if Cobain had a tendency to discuss fame as if it had been a reluctant accident, the events of September 9, 1992, made it clear the band also knew how to revel in the spotlight. Nirvana wasn't above something as commercially crass as the MTV Video Music Awards, but the band most certainly knew how to use it as a tool to their advantage.

When time came for Nirvana to perform, the band surprised MTV—and home viewers—by playing a few bars of "Rape Me." It was a casual drift into the song, and as Cobain repeated the words "rape me," it hit like a middle finger. To a fourteen-year-old watching at home, it was the kind of moment that caused genuine surprise and excitement. *What did he just say? What song was that? That wasn't on* Nevermind, *was it?*

Before there was an answer, and before MTV could carry out its promise to cut to commercial, the band jolted into *Nevermind*'s" "Lithium." The crowd appropriately slam-danced and Grohl and Cobain, back to adhering to the script, shattered their instruments. Novoselic, however, hammed it up, tossing his bass into the air and missing its catch on the way down, playing the plop on the head as more

KURT'S TOP 50 ALBUMS

BUTTHOLE SURFERS
Locust Abortion Technician
(Touch and Go, 1987)
Well before their label run in the 1990s, the Butthole Surfers arrived at an intersection of urban psychedelic noise-rock, hardcore, and post-punk that reached its zenith with *Locust Abortion Technician* right around the time they gelled into an unstoppable and highly influential live act. The LP is a mishmash of sludge-metal, fuzz-punk, horrifying if not hilarious sound bites and samples, and the notorious bulldozer that opened the whole hell-ride (a reinterpretation of Black Sabbath's "Sweet Leaf" retitled "Sweat Loaf") with its giggle-inducing spoken intro. *Locust Abortion Technician* is the quintessential "if you must own one Butthole Surfers record" for casual fans and a desert-island disc for disciples. *AE*

serious than it was. It was vintage Nirvana, packing both a message and juvenile antics.

The perception that Nirvana was sullen, didn't want fame, and, in fact, couldn't handle fame had dogged the group since the early 1990s. It was articulated, with little sensitivity, by *60 Minutes* commenter Andy Rooney in the days after Cobain killed himself. "What would all these young people be doing if they had real problems like a Depression, World War II, or Vietnam?" Rooney declared. "Do they work at all? Are they contributing anything to the world they're taking so much from?"

Rooney was making the same mistake that many outside of Nirvana's demographic committed. Writing off Nirvana as flannel-wearing slackers was the equivalent of dismissing the Beatles as flower-power hippies. Yet Nirvana's image is frozen in time. Further, it was a failure to see that such adult entitlement—the stubborn belief that things in the 1990s were simply better—was the direct root of Nirvana's frustration.

I GOT A NEW COMPLAINT **145**

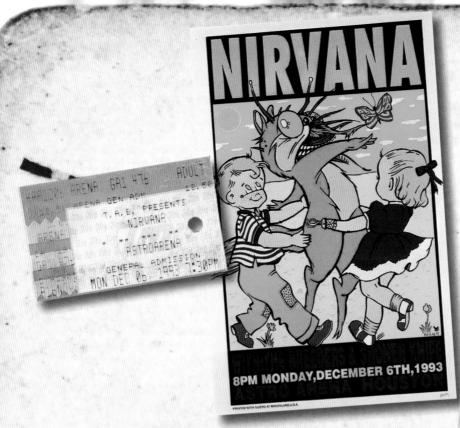

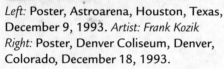

Left: Poster, Astroarena, Houston, Texas, December 9, 1993. *Artist: Frank Kozik*
Right: Poster, Denver Coliseum, Denver, Colorado, December 18, 1993.

KURT'S TOP 50 ALBUMS

BLACK FLAG
Damaged (Unicorn/MCA, 1981; SST, 1982)
Widely considered the consummate American hardcore album, Black Flag's debut full-length introduced their fourth and final singer—one Henry Rollins—and laid down the first and only studio recording of their legendary five-piece lineup. It is simply impossible to understate or underrate this album and its continuing sonic footprint on hardcore punk rock. *Damaged* is America's line of demarcation between punk rock that flirted with hardcore elements and hardcore that resented punk rock's cartoonish condition circa 1981. *AE*

Where some saw a rock 'n' roll trio that sang of boredom, others saw a group that was simply pissed off, following in the tradition of punk-rock rabble-rousers like the Sex Pistols and the Clash.

Selling out was such a hot topic of conversation in the early 1990s because there was growing suspicion that those with money were mishandling it. Foreshadowing the recession-era 2000s, the early 1990s were littered with tales of corporate sweatshops, concerns over the low wages offered by the big chains, and news stories that told of a connection between big oil and the Gulf War. It was a more abstract cause than "make love, not war," and likewise, Nirvana's anger was all over the map.

"I think that if you make money, and you start voting Republican because you'll get tax breaks and they're the party of the rich, I mean, that's sold out," Novoselic said on *Nevermind, It's an Interview*, a promotional CD released by Geffen.

And thus, Nirvana used its appearance at the MTV Video Music Awards to act as something of a Trojan

horse from the underground. It wasn't planned, but the band's target that night ended up being the most extravagant star in rock 'n' roll: Axl Rose. By the time the show was over, Nirvana had taken down the bad boy of 1980s rock, with a little help, of course, from Love, who had goaded Rose into challenging Cobain to a fight.

The story has been well documented in the press and the exact phrasing of the words exchanged varies from article to article, depending on who is being quoted. Audio available online, believed to be recorded in Portland days after the awards, provides perhaps the most colorful descriptions. Everything took place backstage at the Video Music Awards. Love and Cobain were apparently sitting with then three-month-old daughter Frances Bean. As Cobain told it, Love yelled at Rose, "Axl, will you be the godfather of our child?"

Guns N' Roses were established superstars, and while the band had its share of turmoil and expletive-laden songs, at the MTV VMAs that year, GN'R performed

1993 Nirvana T-shirts.
www.WycoVintage.com

KURT'S TOP 50 ALBUMS

FEAR

The Record (Slash, 1982)

Fear was formed by actor and journeyman musician Lee Ving, who had performed with a blues-rock act as a teenager in the 1960s and traveled the country following various muses until giving punk rock a shot with his most notorious musical gesture. Fear gained national fame overnight via a disastrous *Saturday Night Live* appearance on Halloween Night 1981, brokered by friend of the band and constant cheerleader John Belushi in repayment for the band being forced off the soundtrack for the funnyman's also-disastrous film adaptation of the Thomas Berger novel, *Neighbors*. The band's debut gets in, offends and pokes fun, and gets out. Though considered an important hardcore punk document, *The Record* is clearly the work of professionals—or, rather, professional smartasses. *AE*

Below: Poster, Oakland-Alameda County Coliseum Arena, Oakland, California, December 31, 1993.

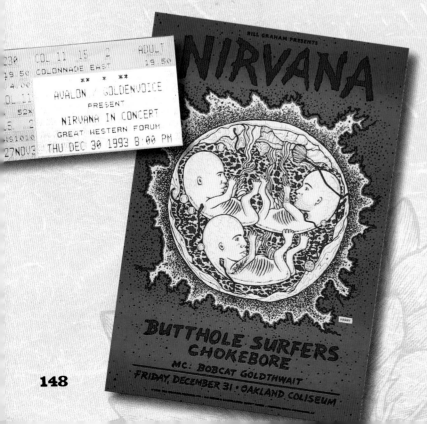

with the regal Elton John, giving a stately, orchestra-enhanced rendition of "November Rain."

It was a performance that Mom and Dad could approve. Using the same promotional platform that GN'R had, Nirvana sought to distance themselves from everyone else who appeared that night. The incident with Rose occurred behind cameras, and Nirvana milked it. Can you, the band seemed to challenge their audience, relate to such extravagance?

Cobain spoke of Rose being surrounded by bodyguards, adding that he was "shaking" and that Rose warned him that he "better keep your wife's mouth shut." Cobain, mocking Rose's out-of-date machismo, sarcastically yelled "Shut up, bitch," to Love. It escalated still: "Are you a model?" Rose's girlfriend Stephanie Seymour asked Love, to which she shushed everyone up by replying, "No. Are you a brain surgeon?"

It all furthered Nirvana's "us against them" mentality, and while the two bands couldn't have looked more different, Nirvana proved that night to be far more clever at self-promotion. Rose was only a few years removed from the outlaw status Nirvana was now enjoying, and his band was even employed by the same record label. Yet Nirvana, having sprung from independent Sub Pop, was challenging the established order while waving the flag for a world of music most MTV viewers had not yet discovered even after the success of *Nevermind*.

As the 1990s gave way to the 2000s, the rise in file sharing made a direct hit on the bottom line of major labels, making it more and more likely that independent acts and unknown artists could find an audience. In 1992, however, the path to the mass populace was still through the gatekeepers that were the major record labels. Nirvana already had a hit album, showing that the gates could be kicked wide open.

Two months after the MTV awards Nirvana released *Incesticide*, which drove the latter point home. The album, a stop-gap collection of odds and ends, is an uncomfortable listen at times—its sound is muddled and production is shoddy. Word was the band wanted to clean the songs up, but whoever decided against it—whether Nirvana or Geffen—had made the right call (Cross, in his biography, reported that the band acquiesced when it was given control over the artwork and presentation).

Kurt Cobain on stage at Inglewood, California, December 30, 1993. *Henry Diltz/Corbis*

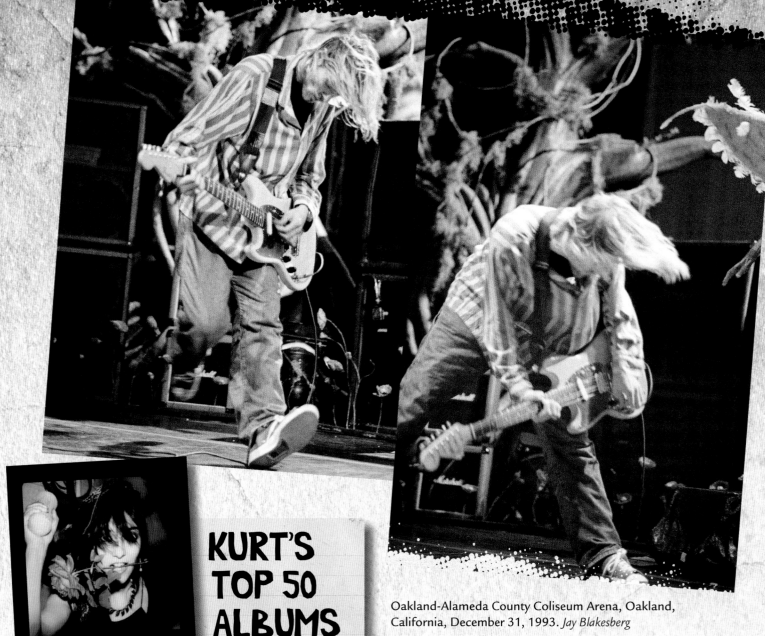

Oakland-Alameda County Coliseum Arena, Oakland, California, December 31, 1993. *Jay Blakesberg*

KURT'S TOP 50 ALBUMS

PUBLIC IMAGE LTD

The Flowers of Romance

(Virgin/Warner Bros., 1981)

PiL's third album is one of the most brazenly anti-commercial major-label records this side of Lou Reed's *Metal Machine Music*. Aside from tons of drums, *The Flowers of Romance* has Keith Levene indulging his newfound obsession with modulating synths and tone generators and often running his guitar through them (when the instrument is present at all). Other decidedly *musique concrète* elements like a recorded wristwatch, phased in and out opera singing, and a banjo head are utilized, and John Lydon's vocals are at their anti-pop apex. Possibly the most efficient room-emptier to be found in the cutout bin, it's a real head-scratcher. *AE*

Music critics of the time were hip to independent labels like Sub Pop and Touch and Go, but most teens had nothing that sounded as unkempt as *Incesticide* in their collections. Furthermore, it was an introduction to heretofore unknown bands such as Scotland's sex-obsessed, pop-rock humorists the Vaselines. If Nirvana was going big, they were bringing others with them.

"What's good is a lot of really good underground bands are gonna get really good distribution and some money," Novoselic optimistically told *NME* in early 1992. "In a best case scenario, a lot of these bands' attitude and values can rub off on mainstream culture."

In early 1993, Nirvana set out to do more than challenge mainstream culture. The band embarked on a calculated risk that would put it directly in the line

KURT'S TOP 50 ALBUMS

MARINE GIRLS
Beach Party (Whaam!, 1982)
This first-wave U.K. DIY outfit came off like a more-structured Raincoats and is often referred to as "post-punk" when in fact they played an early form of twee-pop that would launch as a movement a bit later thanks to NME's C86 compilation tape (free with the magazine). It's a pleasant and delightfully catchy affair, but Marine Girls will forever be better known as the first band of Tracey Thorn, who would disband Marine Girls in 1983 and form the highly successful Everything But the Girl with then-boyfriend Ben Watts. AE

of fire. They were, to be blunt, setting themselves up for a fight.

Steve Albini was not the obvious choice to produce the follow-up to the multimillion-selling *Nevermind*. A staunch opponent of the major label system, he was an underground producer who preferred to keep it that way and an artist who had already expressed disgust at the alternative rock craze sweeping the nation.

Albini's best-known band, Big Black, took a scorched-earth approach to songcraft. Songs were crude—guitars chugged and bass notes rattled like metal chains—as if formed with dysfunctional, broken instruments. This was the rare garage band that actually sounded as if it were constructing songs largely with tools one could find in a garage.

Albini had worked with artists Cobain revered, namely the Pixies, whose loud/soft dynamics and knack for melody laid the foundation for all things Nirvana. *Surfer Rosa*, the band's Albini-produced album, was harsh, raw, and precise—instruments were recorded in such a way that they seemed to progress on separate but parallel fronts.

And the man was outspoken. "Unremarkable" was the one-word assessment Albini once leveled at Nirvana, though its original source is difficult to trace. In a December 1992 interview with the *Chicago Tribune*—months before he would spend a couple weeks with Nirvana—Albini wasn't subtle in his take on the current music scene. He dismissed Sonic Youth's Thurston Moore as having become part of the "shyster process" for having worked with Geffen. It was, in fact, the pavement-scraping noise-rock of Sonic Youth that Cobain often cited as his own inspiration for inking a deal with Geffen. In the same article, Albini took time out to slam the rock bands from his own city that were starting to gain attention.

"The way the music scene is operating these days, I don't want to be associated with it," Albini said. "I don't like people thinking of me in the same way they think of the Smashing Pumpkins or Urge Overkill or any of these other hype-happy, B.S., insubstantial bands from Chicago."

Opposite: Oakland-Alameda County Coliseum Arena, Oakland, California, December 31, 1993. *Jay Blakesberg*

THE GEAR THAT MADE GRUNGE FAMOUS

by Alan di Perna

Life isn't easy for left-handed electric guitarists like Kurt Cobain. Left-handed instruments are pretty hard to find. Guitar companies don't manufacture all that many, so lefties must often settle for whatever is available. You can try flipping a right-handed guitar upside down, as Jimi Hendrix did, but then your left hand and arm are very likely to knock into the tone and volume controls, messing up your sound. Guitars with toggle switches or rocker panels can suddenly go dead in the middle of a performance—an embarrassing experience.

Cobain tried the upside-down approach early on, using a cheapie right-handed Sears bass to make his earliest known amateur recordings at the home of his aunt, Mari Earl. He also acquired a 1960s-vintage, right-handed Mosrite Gospel fairly early in his career, and owned several other right-handed guitars as well, including a Japanese-made Epiphone ET-270 from the 1970s. But, eventually, he shifted his attention to left-handed guitars.

Now, if you don't have a lot of money to spend on a left-handed guitar—which was Cobain's financial situation for much of his life as a musician—an already meager realm of possibilities shrinks even further. *And* if you're prone, as was Cobain, to smash your guitars onstage, you must deal with the perpetual challenge of finding replacement instruments and parts.

Given all of these limitations, Cobain's choice of guitars during his career was both pragmatic and shrewd. For the most part he favored Fender guitars—a wise choice for a guitar smasher. Fenders are built to take a beating in the first place, and Leo Fender designed the things to be easily repairable when they do get broken. Fender's bolt-on neck design makes it relatively easy to reattach severed necks and to recycle the guitar parts that litter the stage after a performance. And the scratch-plate pickup assembly design on several Fender models affords easy access to a guitar's electronic guts for repairs.

Cobain gravitated toward the cheaper end of the Fender line, again in keeping with budget limitations during the early phases of his career as well as his overall punk rock aesthetic. But even within the "affordable" range, he chose wisely.

One of his main guitars, perhaps the instrument most central to his work with Nirvana, was a left-handed, sunburst 1965 Fender Jaguar that he acquired in the summer of 1991. While the Jaguar had been Fender's most expensive guitar when it was first introduced in 1962, it never achieved the popularity of models like the Stratocaster and Telecaster and was discontinued in 1975. Which means that used Jags (today we call them vintage) were a great bargain in the early 1990s when Nirvana was coming up.

And the Jaguar had great punk rock cred, stemming from its use by Tom Verlaine of the seminal 1970s punk band Television and numerous 1990s alternative rockers, including Sonic Youth and My Bloody Valentine. All of this, combined with Cobain's association with the instrument, would greatly increase the value of vintage Jags in years to come. Cobain owned at least one other Jaguar, a 1964, and he would generally replace the

Opposite: Cobain with his sunburst 1965 Fender Jaguar at the Astoria, London, May 11, 1991. He purchased this left-handed Jaguar during the summer of 1991. It would become one of his main guitars. *Ian Dickson/ Redferns/Getty Images*

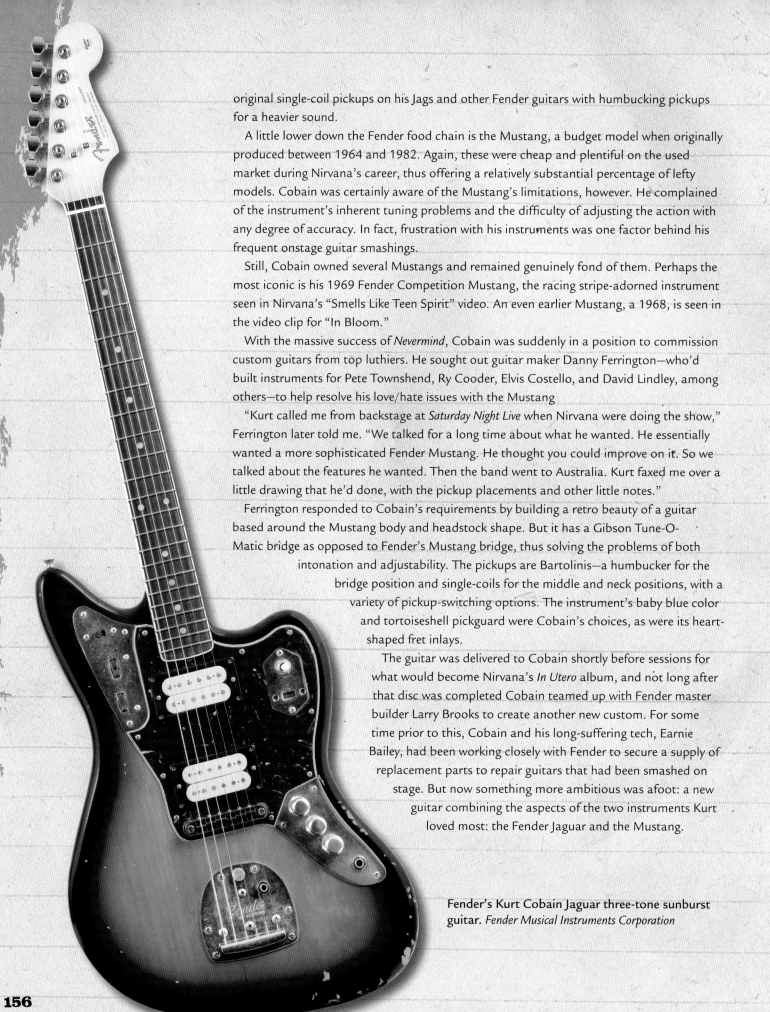

original single-coil pickups on his Jags and other Fender guitars with humbucking pickups for a heavier sound.

A little lower down the Fender food chain is the Mustang, a budget model when originally produced between 1964 and 1982. Again, these were cheap and plentiful on the used market during Nirvana's career, thus offering a relatively substantial percentage of lefty models. Cobain was certainly aware of the Mustang's limitations, however. He complained of the instrument's inherent tuning problems and the difficulty of adjusting the action with any degree of accuracy. In fact, frustration with his instruments was one factor behind his frequent onstage guitar smashings.

Still, Cobain owned several Mustangs and remained genuinely fond of them. Perhaps the most iconic is his 1969 Fender Competition Mustang, the racing stripe-adorned instrument seen in Nirvana's "Smells Like Teen Spirit" video. An even earlier Mustang, a 1968, is seen in the video clip for "In Bloom."

With the massive success of *Nevermind*, Cobain was suddenly in a position to commission custom guitars from top luthiers. He sought out guitar maker Danny Ferrington—who'd built instruments for Pete Townshend, Ry Cooder, Elvis Costello, and David Lindley, among others—to help resolve his love/hate issues with the Mustang

"Kurt called me from backstage at *Saturday Night Live* when Nirvana were doing the show," Ferrington later told me. "We talked for a long time about what he wanted. He essentially wanted a more sophisticated Fender Mustang. He thought you could improve on it. So we talked about the features he wanted. Then the band went to Australia. Kurt faxed me over a little drawing that he'd done, with the pickup placements and other little notes."

Ferrington responded to Cobain's requirements by building a retro beauty of a guitar based around the Mustang body and headstock shape. But it has a Gibson Tune-O-Matic bridge as opposed to Fender's Mustang bridge, thus solving the problems of both intonation and adjustability. The pickups are Bartolinis—a humbucker for the bridge position and single-coils for the middle and neck positions, with a variety of pickup-switching options. The instrument's baby blue color and tortoiseshell pickguard were Cobain's choices, as were its heart-shaped fret inlays.

The guitar was delivered to Cobain shortly before sessions for what would become Nirvana's *In Utero* album, and not long after that disc was completed Cobain teamed up with Fender master builder Larry Brooks to create another new custom. For some time prior to this, Cobain and his long-suffering tech, Earnie Bailey, had been working closely with Fender to secure a supply of replacement parts to repair guitars that had been smashed on stage. But now something more ambitious was afoot: a new guitar combining the aspects of the two instruments Kurt loved most: the Fender Jaguar and the Mustang.

Fender's Kurt Cobain Jaguar three-tone sunburst guitar. *Fender Musical Instruments Corporation*

Cobain with one of his Fender Mustang guitars.
Kevin Mazur Archive 1/WireImage/Getty Images

To illustrate to Brooks what he had in mind, Cobain took Polaroid photos of a Mustang and a Jaguar, cut the photos in half and pasted them together in a way that combined the upper part of the Mustang body with the lower portion of the Jaguar body. The resultant hybrid was named the Jagstang, an instrument with an alder body, a DiMarzio H-3 humbucker in the bridge position, and a single-coil Fender Texas Special pickup in the neck position. At Cobain's request, Brooks used stock Mustang hardware from Japan, where the guitars were still in production at the time. Bailey later switched the bridge to a Tune-O-Matic.

Like Ferrington, Brooks told me he enjoyed working with Cobain, describing him as "very soft-spoken and very gentle. He was easy to work with. He knew what he wanted, but at the same time he was very open-minded. It took less time to design and build the guitar than it does just to communicate with some other artists."

Cobain ordered two Jagstangs, one in blue and one in red. The blue instrument was used on Nirvana's 1993 tour. Fender were about to ship the red one when news reached them of Cobain's death.

Despite his love for Jaguars, Mustangs, and even Musicmasters (another affordable Fender model), Cobain was by no means averse to more mainstream Fenders like the Stratocaster and Telecaster. He owned several Strats—preferring the Japanese-made models because of their smaller frets—and at least one Strat copy made by Fernandez. He also had a 1993 Fender Custom Telecaster that he favored for songwriting and personal use. Along with these, Cobain owned, played, and smashed a number of Univox Hi-Fliers, a cheap guitar modeled after Mosrite solidbodies like Cobain's early Gospel model.

As for acoustic guitars, Cobain didn't own very many during his lifetime. The earliest known was a Stella Harmony 12-string, purchased at a pawn shop in 1989 for about thirty bucks and most famously used on Nirvana's song "Polly." While technically a 12-string, the guitar only had 5 nylon strings on it

VANDALISM:
BEAUTIFUL AS A ROCK
IN A COP'S FACE

Courtesy of the Feedback Office of Anti-Public Relations

during much of its time with Cobain. Following *Nevermind*'s multiplatinum ascent, Cobain moved up to an Epiphone Texan, the same model Paul McCartney used to record "Yesterday." Cobain's Texan was a right-handed guitar adapted for lefty use (much easier on an acoustic than on an electric guitar) and adorned—somewhat ironically, it's presumed—with a sticker that read "Nixon Now."

The final acoustic guitar of Cobain's brief life was a Martin D-18E that he purchased at Voltage Guitar in Los Angeles in the fall of 1993. Inadvertently, most likely, he'd picked quite a rare one. Only 302 D-18s were ever made. The guitar, Martin's first attempt at an electrified acoustic guitar, was introduced in 1958 and discontinued in 1959.

"I don't believe he had any idea of how rare it was before he bought it," Bailey told me. "Kurt was neither a collector nor a connoisseur of rare guitars. I think he saw the D-18E as an oddity, hoping it would sound as good as it looked."

Bailey supplemented the guitar's original DeArmond pickups with Bartolini 3AVs. "Kurt first became interested in that pickup when he saw Peter Buck using one and really liked the sound," said the guitar tech.

The D-18E was most famously played by Cobain during Nirvana's appearance on MTV's *Unplugged* program. And actually, Cobain was rather well plugged-in for his *Unplugged* performance. His Martin was routed through a series of effects pedals into his much-loved 1982 Fender Twin Reverb, an amp he'd also used on *In Utero* sessions. Another amplifier heavily favored during Nirvana's mainstream heyday, including some *Nevermind* sessions, was a Mesa Boogie Studio Preamp, routed through a variety of power amp and speaker cab combinations.

As for effects, the classic grunge distortion sound that Cobain did much to originate and popularize was generated by a number of different pedals, including the Electro-Harmonix Big Muff, ProCo Rat, and a range of BOSS distortion units. And that watery Nirvana chorus sound, which quickly became another grunge guitar staple, was principally created by a variety of Electro-Harmonix pedals, including the Small Clone chorus, EchoFlanger, and PolyChorus.

Krist Novoselic, for his part, played Ibanez Black Eagle and Roadster basses, as well as Gibson Ripper, RD, and Thunderbird IV basses, principally through an Ampeg SVT400T amp. Like Kurt, he was fond of the ProCo Rat, which he'd employ for more distorted bass timbres. For *MTV Unplugged*, Krist played a rented Guild B30E semi-acoustic bass and a Dobren accordion that belonged to Kurt.

Right: **Fender's Kurt Cobain left-handed Mustang in Sonic Blue.** *Fender Musical Instruments Corporation* *Opposite:* **Cobain in 1991 with one of the several left-handed fender Stratocasters he owned over the years.** *Kevin Estrada*

Backstage passs, *In Utero* Tour, 1993-1994. *Kevin Estrada*

Albini's final summation of the current pop landscape? "I've got a strong enough distaste for what's going on out there that I don't want to enter the fray."

His hiring by Nirvana was largely seen as a sign that the band wanted to escape the very fray that Albini was hoping to avoid. It was a choice by Nirvana to not just reconnect with its punk rock roots, but make that connection a concrete one.

This theme would spill over from the recording process to Nirvana's tours in support of *In Utero*, on which the band shunned major label packaged tours to pair up with lesser-known idols. Further distancing themselves from their major label peers, Nirvana tapped the hippy-metal of the Meat Puppets and the bleeding-heart relentlessness of Jawbreaker.

Long before any tickets were sold, there were doubts that *In Utero* would even see the light of day. Before recording began, Nirvana members were actively distancing themselves from the larger-than-life rock of *Nevermind*, expressing a desire to strip it down and show the band's guts. They were slyly crafting a storyline that placed Nirvana on a mission to shed some of its major label skin.

"We're actually going to spend less money," Novoselic told Australia's *Sun-Herald Magazine* in early 1992, when *Nevermind* was still gaining in momentum. Implying the band was already plotting a reversal of course, he added,

"People are prone to yell sell-out and we'd yell sell-out ourselves. We wouldn't be comfortable with a slick, distilled record."

Grohl latter summarized his issues with *Nevermind*. "*Nevermind*'s only flaw was that it had no flaws," he told *Q* magazine. "Play it alongside our live tapes and it's a sharp, thin thing compared to this boom, this rumble . . . *In Utero* is boom and rumble, man."

In Utero was recorded in a two-week span at the rurally situated Pachyderm Studio in Cannon Falls, Minnesota, about thirty-five miles from the Twin Cities. Studio costs were initially pegged at $17,000 by Cobain, but the final cost was around $25,000. Albini charged a flat fee of $100,000 and declined a royalty.

Representatives from Geffen were strictly forbidden from visiting the studio, and Cobain told the *New York Times* that all the vocals for *In Utero* were done in one seven-hour marathon session, as opposed to the multiple days of vocal work for *Nevermind*. The setup was relatively simple. The band played live in a room full of mics.

Geffen was happy to indulge Nirvana in its wishes to work with Albini, but there were hints they hoped that it was all a lark. "Our A&R man at the time, Gary Gersh, was freaking out," Grohl told *Q*. "I said, 'Gary, man, don't be so afraid, the record will turn out great!' He said, 'Oh, I'm not afraid, go ahead, bring me back the best you can do.' It was like, Go and have your fun, then we'll get another producer and make the *real* album."

Cobain had said he wanted *In Utero* to reflect Nirvana in its truest form. "By listening to those records," Cobain told *Request*, referring to Albini's past work, "I realized something that I had been trying to prove for like three years. Ever since we started recording, I've always thought that it would be really logical to record with a lot of microphones to get an ambience from the room. It just seems obvious to me that if you want it to sound like you're standing right next to the band, if you want that live feeling, then you have to use a lot of microphones."

After leaving Minnesota, the battles started. A war of words erupted among Albini, Nirvana, and Gersh. Albini expressed doubts that Geffen would release the album. Cobain at times wavered in his confidence in the work, and the *Chicago Tribune*

Kurt Cobain and Nirvana play the Seattle Arena, Seattle, Washington, January 7, 1994. The concert would be the band's last American performance. *Kevin Estrada*

KURT'S TOP 50 ALBUMS

PUBLIC ENEMY
It Takes a Nation of Millions to Hold Us Back
(Def Jam, 1988)
A loud, propulsive, and bombastic masterpiece of hip-hop's initial golden era, Public Enemy's sophomore breakthrough gave the world "She Watch Channel Zero," "Night of the Living Baseheads," "Bring the Noise," "Don't Believe the Hype," and the powerhouse "Rebel Without a Pause." *AE*

Above: Poster, Pacific National Exhibition Forum, Vancouver, British Columbia, Canada, January 3, 1994.
Right: Kurt Cobain and Nirvana play the Seattle Arena, Seattle, Washington, January 7, 1994. The concert would be the band's last American performance.
Kevin Estrada

KURT'S TOP 50 ALBUMS

DAVID BOWIE

The Man Who Sold the World (Mercury, 1970)
This LP rivals Bowie's Eno-era albums of the late-1970s as his most important work of the decade, and perhaps his career. It is Bowie's heaviest album by a good measure, and several tracks (particularly "Black Country Rock" and "Running Gun Blues") owe an obvious debt to Led Zeppelin, Black Sabbath, Atomic Rooster, and other early metal pioneers. It is also the thematically darkest album of his early-1970s reinvention era. *The Man Who Sold the World* is a hard-rock/proto-metal necessity (it's also been cited as the first glam record). Nirvana would, of course, include the title track on their 1993 *MTV Unplugged in New York* release. *AE*

in April 1993 reported that a "source close to the band" deemed it "unreleasable."

Albini fanned the flames. He was quoted in *Request* saying, "I don't think that all the pussies and wimps who liked the last album will ever like this one." Grohl told *Q*, "I happen to love Steve Albini. He really prides himself on being the biggest dick you ever met in your life and he does a good job of it."

Gersh told the *Los Angeles Times* that he gave the band feedback, "but I made it clear from the beginning that we'd put out the record regardless." An article in *Newsweek* intensified matters by raising further suspicion about the album's prospects at seeing the light of day. Nirvana responded with a full-page ad in *Billboard* declaring that band and label were getting along just swimmingly.

Cobain said issues he had with the Albini tapes were solved in mixing and mastering. Two *In Utero* songs ("Heart-Shaped Box" and "All Apologies") were ultimately remixed by R.E.M. producer Scott Litt. To use Grohl's parlance, the Litt remixes smoothed out some of the "boom and rumble."

"Those tapes we took away from the studio sounded very different when we played them at home," Cobain told *Q*. "For three weeks, none of us could work out what was wrong and we didn't know what the fuck we were going to do. Then we realized it was the vocals and the bass weren't loud enough. The mixing we'd done with Steve Albini was so fast it was ridiculous, about one hour per track."

Albini disowned the final product. "I'm not happy with the way that record sounds in its released state," he told the *Chicago Tribune*. Cobain, meanwhile, eventually told *Request* that "I wasn't half as proud of *Nevermind* as I am of this record. We intentionally made an aggressive record."

While *In Utero* is unmistakably Nirvana, it is claustrophobic at times. Second song "Scentless Apprentice" ends with Cobain screaming "Go awaaaaaaaay," his voice sounding so hoarse one can practically picture the blood beginning to swell inside his vocal cords. "Radio Friendly Unit Shifter" is all rough edges and alarming guitars, with feedback ringing at every turn.

The album's title was also a sign of Nirvana's humor, a side of the band often overlooked. Cobain opened the album with the jabbing refrain, "Teenage angst has paid off well/Now I'm old and bored," and "Pennyroyal Tea" was full of colorful images ("cherry-flavored antacids") that satirized the haves and have-nots.

But if *Nevermind* was designed to be blasted from car windows, *In Utero* offered more nuanced abrasion. "Milk It" is riddled with demented guitar notes, which poke at the listener and melody with a needling persistence, whereas "Dumb" was Nirvana's attempt at writing a borderline folk song.

The album debuted at No. 1 on the U.S. pop charts, and the band easily sold out seven to nine thousand–capacity venues. Ultimately, though, sales wouldn't measure up to *Nevermind*. As of early 2013, *Nevermind* had sold 9 million copies in the United States according to SoundScan, compared to *In Utero*'s 4.2 million.

Nirvana expected as much. "I don't have high hopes of staying up in the charts. Meat Loaf is so obviously more talented than I am," Cobain joked to the *New York Times* (again, the humor).

But if the band had settled its differences with Albini by the time the album was released, the group still wasn't making things easier on its more casual fans. *In Utero* tour dates often ended with a mini acoustic set, complete with haunting Appalachian folk stalker "Where Did You Sleep Last Night" (more commonly known as "In the Pines" back in its day).

It was far removed from the teenage angst of *Nevermind*, a point made clear by the first single and video. Largely conceived by Cobain, the video was a collage of nightmare images—a fetus from a tree, Jesus wearing a Santa hat while being crucified, a little girl in KKK garb, and Jesus lying in a hospital bed. If the video for "Smells Like Teen Spirit" was designed to capture high school alienation, "Heart-Shaped Box" was art-house material for a college thesis.

Released at a time when grunge copycats Stone Temple Pilots had a Top 10 album—and the Whitney Houston–led soundtrack to *The Bodyguard* was still a force—*In Utero* was a statement that Nirvana would not be confined by the Seattle-bred sound. What's more, the very public battles with Albini and Geffen signified, whether justly or not, that this was a band taking

control of its destiny and bringing the DIY aesthetic into the major label system.

Long before the advent of YouTube and social networking, which allowed artists greater control over their own image and sound, *In Utero* was a signifier to fans that their beloved band could operate without the corporate watchdogs interfering—at least too much—even if it lost them some followers in the process. The sense that Geffen would have ultimately preferred a producer other than Albini has never really been refuted. Years later, in 2002, when the label compiled a single-CD history of the band, *In Utero*-cut "Pennyroyal Tea" made the collection, but it was the Scott Litt version, not the Albini mix. The differences were subtle, but they were there. Gone was Cobain's cough that opened the song on *In Utero*, and the song's lighter parts were warmer, less off-kilter. The main riff was also sharper on the original. With Albini's take, it was as if one could hear the electrical currents shoot between the guitar and amp, whereas the Litt mix made it louder, less defined.

Artistically, Nirvana in 1993 had won what it fought for. Any perceived good fortune, though, would take a rather sudden turn in the months after the release of *In Utero*.

The antagonistic natures of Nirvana and Cobain didn't always result in artistic triumphs. Drugs, overdoses, police reports, media paranoia, and an increasing obsession with firearms that started in 1993 became as much a part of Nirvana's story as the music. And yet, amid the distractions and the dysfunction, there were moments of musical release that persuaded fans everything was in its right place. The November 1993 taping of *MTV Unplugged in New York* was one such instance. Stories later emerged that the entire concert was mired in doubt, as Cobain appeared at the studios in the midst of a withdrawal, disinterested in talking to anyone.

What home viewers saw a month later when MTV aired the special was a singer who seemed mildly disenchanted in the environment's formal trappings. As if to underscore his misgivings in what had already become a predictable format for MTV, Cobain denied the crowd the band's latest single, "Heart-Shaped Box," and its biggest hit, "Smells Like Teen Spirit." Instead, he brought out heroes the Meat Puppets to play one of the latter's songs, covered David Bowie's "The Man Who Sold the World," spoke fondly of Scotland's Vaselines,

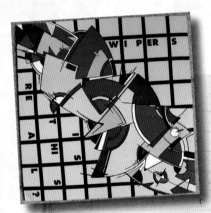

KURT'S TOP 50 ALBUMS

WIPERS

Is This Real? (Park Avenue/Sub Pop, 1980/1993) Nirvana covered two songs ("Return of the Rat" and "D-7") from the debut album by brilliant Portland post-punk band, The Wipers, led by the immensely talented and driven Greg Sage. Sub Pop reissued *Is This Real?* in 1993 with bonus tracks. Imagine a sort of Pacific Northwest version of early–Mission of Burma without the avant-overtones, and that's only part of the way there. Essential. *AE*

Poster, Pabellón de Deportes del Real Madrid, Madrid, Spain, February 9, 1994.

and spent much of his between-song chatter discussing which song to play. Cameras routinely showed Grohl shrugging, as the band looked to have little clue as to which direction Cobain would lead them.

This was Nirvana playing the game and not playing it, all at the same time. The set ended not with a bang, but with the hushed, stark fascination of "Where Did You Sleep Last Night." Cobain brushed off Grohl's attempts to play "Sliver," and joked with the crowd about MTV not wanting the band to play "Rape Me."

Cobain, swiveling in his chair and with his voice at its most crackling and fragile, was riveting. Between songs, he appeared stoned, but in the midst of them, he was lucid. Was he out of it, or giving the network and his mainstream fans the middle finger? Consider that he opened the show not with a hello, but an immediate brushoff to those watching. "This is off our first record," he said to introduce "About a Girl." "Most people don't own it."

Yet the punk rock antics in front of the camera were masking a tragic soap opera behind them. Cobain and Love's reputation as heroin addicts was formalized for the world in a 1992 *Vanity Fair* article by Lynn Hirschberg. Cobain, discussing the events after an appearance on *Saturday Night Live*, stated, "Then we got high and went to 'S.N.L.' After that, I did heroin for a couple of months." Love at the time was pregnant with Frances Bean.

Statements, denials, and an outright mistrust of the media followed. From that day forward, Cobain insisted that his record label listen in and tape most interviews with the press, should he ever be misquoted, and Cobain and Love briefly had to fight the city of Los Angeles for custody of Frances Bean. Months after the *Vanity Fair* article, Cobain told the *Los Angeles Times* that he was through with drugs. "I don't want my daughter to grow up and someday be hassled by kids at school," he said. "I don't want people telling her that her parents were junkies."

Tickets, European Tour, Winter 1994.

KURT'S TOP 50 ALBUMS

WIPERS

Youth of America (Park Avenue, 1981)
An experimental reaction to the traditional songcraft of most punk rock, American post-punk, and early hardcore, the amazing title track is over ten minutes long and was treated to a breathtaking cover version by the Melvins on their 2001 album, *Electroretard*. Sonic Youth's Thurston Moore cites this album as a big influence, and he covered "Pushing the Extreme" for the Wipers tribute album *14 Songs for Greg Sage and The Wipers*, released on Tim/Kerr Records in 1992. *AE*

Unfortunately, there was constant evidence that Cobain was anything but clean. The first sign of major trouble came in the summer of 1993, after *In Utero* was recorded but before it was released. In July, the *Seattle Times*—and then MTV—picked up a story that police had responded to a domestic disturbance call at the Cobain residence.

Cobain was arrested for alleged assault and released on $950 bail after three hours in jail. Charges were never pressed. "Kurt is not violent, he is not a wife-beater, we are the most compatible people on earth," Love told the *Seattle Times*. "It started because we were playing loud music in our garage and we live in a quiet neighborhood. All of a sudden there were sirens and, like, three cop cars, six cops in the house."

The story didn't end there. Love was said to have thrown juice in Cobain's face, and Cobain was said to have thrown her to the ground. Police also seized three guns: "a Beretta .380, a Taurus .380 and a Colt AR-15—

KURT'S TOP 50 ALBUMS

WIPERS

Over the Edge (Brain Eater, 1983)
Much of this third album is covered in guitar distortion and features a return to more hook-oriented songwriting that foreshadowed the late-1980s/early-1990s indie-rock explosion with great prescience. The single "Romeo" got modest airplay at forward-thinking stations, making *Over the Edge* the first Wipers album to garner any national acceptance. Hole covered the title track in 1990. The Wipers broke their rule of little-to-no live performing when they toured extensively in support of this album. *AE*

Tickets, European Tour, Winter 1994.

as well as ammunition clips for the guns," according to the *Seattle Times*. Love admitted that the argument started over the presence of the firearms, which she did not want in the house.

This was one of the first major public hints that Cobain's rebellious streak had a darker undercurrent. He spoke to *Request* about his gun ownership and need for security. "I have a baby and wife to protect," he said. "Things like that happen. People come into your house, not to steal your stereo, but to rape your wife and sodomize your baby. I just couldn't survive something like that. There's no way I could ever live with myself without trying to get revenge on that person and putting him out of his misery."

The *Request* article was released in the fall of 1993. The next few months in Nirvana history focused almost exclusively on the misery—real or perceived—of its front man. As the *In Utero* tour extended into 1994 and headed overseas, talk of Nirvana headlining the 1994 edition of Lollapalooza increased.

Then it all went horribly wrong. In March 1994, Cobain was rushed to a hospital in Rome after falling into a drug-induced coma. Initial news reports in the United States declared Cobain dead, and Italian news agency ANSA said Cobain's coma was triggered by a deadly combination of sedatives and champagne. Love spoke extensively of finding Cobain passed out and blue in the face in their Rome hotel room. This was a suicide attempt, Love would later reveal, complete with a note from Cobain. Details were supposedly kept secret out of fear of child services taking Frances Bean away from the couple if the severity of the situation became public knowledge.

Cobain recovered, but only to find police at his home near Seattle a week later. On March 18, Cobain, rumored to be back on heroin, locked himself in a room. Police found him with three pistols, a rifle, and twenty-five boxes of ammunition, according to the *Los Angeles Times*.

What followed over the next few weeks was chronicled in Charles R. Cross' *Heavier Than Heaven*, and it is some of the most distressing news in modern rock history. Interventions were staged and friends and colleagues pleaded with Cobain to enter rehab. "This has got to end," Cross wrote of Love screaming at Cobain at one of his final interventions. "You have to be a good daddy."

Cobain could barely be a good band member. On April 6, any hope of Nirvana subverting the Lollapalooza machine that summer was over. The band's summer tour dates were off. Worse, the band, according to numerous media outlets, had broken up. "They've been on the verge of breaking up forever and this doesn't sound more serious than the other 43,000 times," an unnamed band source told the *Los Angeles Times*. "This could be a signal from the other members of the band that Kurt needs to focus on taking better care of himself."

It was too late. Cobain was already dead. He had shot himself in the head on April 5 at his Washington home. As the media was wondering whether or not the band had broken up, those closest to Cobain were wondering where he was—and they feared the worst. Days earlier he had embarked on what would be the final battle of his life.

On March 28, Cobain had checked into Exodus, a recovery program in Marina del Rey, California. Friends visited, Love expressed elation, and it seemed that perhaps Cobain was serious about coming clean. Three days later he hopped a fence and left the facility. Rumors and supposed sightings followed. He went back to Seattle and was, for all intents and purposes, lost. One report had him nearly overdosed, left for dead by drug dealers in a car. Other reports had him asking a friend to buy him a shotgun.

Love, meanwhile, was in Los Angeles where she hired a private investigator to track him down. Before Cobain would be found dead, she conducted an interview with the *Los Angeles Times*, crying while a Narcotics Anonymous handbook sat beside her.

Love told the *Times*'s Robert Hilburn of kicking a photographer in Rome who was about to take a "ghoulish" shot of Cobain on a stretcher with tubes in his nose. She said she regretted it: "I wish Kurt could have seen [a photo of himself] because if he had, he never would get into that situation again."

Cobain's body was found April 8, 1994, at 8:30 a.m. by an electrician at the musician's Seattle-area home. He was said to be dead for at least a day, and was ultimately believed to have shot himself on April 5. The electrician called a local radio station and news spread before family could be notified—or the body could be properly identified.

Later on Friday, the King County medical examiner's office released a statement: "An autopsy has shown Kurt Cobain died of a shotgun wound to the head and at this time the wound appears to be self-inflicted."

He left a note.

Love read it at the funeral proceedings. In it, Cobain compared himself to Queen's Freddie Mercury, an artist who "seemed to love, relish in the love and adoration from the crowd. Which is something I totally admire and envy." He spoke of love for his daughter, and of looking in awe at the innocence of Frances Bean, but added, "I can't stand the thought of Frances becoming the miserable, self-destructive, death-rocker that I've become."

Cobain ended with a quote from Neil Young's "Hey Hey, My My (Into the Black)": "It's better to burn out

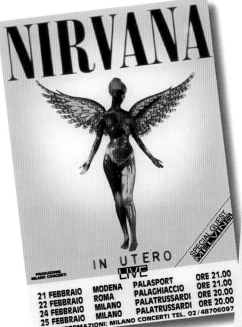

Left: Poster, Italian Tour, Spring 1994.
Above: Poster, Palaghiaccio, Marino, Italy, February 22, 1994. Artist: Alessandro Locchi
Below: Poster, German Tour, Spring 1994.

KURT'S TOP 50 ALBUMS

MAZZY STAR
She Hangs Brightly (Rough Trade/Capitol, 1990)
An extension of the SST band Opal, with the crucial addition of Hope Sandoval on vocals, Mazzy Star has origins in L.A.'s "paisley underground" movement of the 1980s, but the gauzy, hypnotic atmosphere and semi-shoe-gaze guitar work timestamps *She Hangs Brightly* at the end of the day. An immersion-friendly and often gorgeous album that takes a few spins to really unpack its special subtleties, Mazzy Star's debut would collect a gradual cult following over the years, but the band's next album, 1993's *So Tonight That I Might See*, would give them a minor hit with the single "Fade Into You." *AE*

Opposite: Kurt Cobain onstage at the Palasport, Modena, Italy, February 21, 1994, playing his Fender Mustang. *Raffaella Cavalieri/Redferns/Getty Images*

KURT'S TOP 50 ALBUMS

SWANS

Young God EP (K 422 Records, 1984)
Ending Cobain's list of fifty favorite "albums" is this four-track EP, the fourth release from New York City's finest purveyors of sonic brutalization, degradation, and experimentation. *Young God* marks the band's use of a metal table and chains to add percussion, and the title track is told from the point of view of serial killer Ed Gein. The EP would sell over a thousand copies in its first year, which, relative to the music at hand, is mind-blowing and just plain *weird*. AE

than to fade away." Love scolded the crowd, as if she alone would be the one delivering the lesson in all of this. "Don't remember this because this is a fucking lie."

After Cobain's death, Capitol CEO Gary Gersh, who had signed Nirvana to Geffen, told the *Los Angeles Times*, "When people look back over the years at the industry, I believe there will be a pre-Nirvana business and a post-Nirvana business. The group's *Nevermind* album will be looked back on as a seminal record in the history of rock."

Pearl Jam's Eddie Vedder seemed to hear both Love and Gersh. Just days after Cobain's death Pearl Jam appeared on *Saturday Night Live* and briefly performed "Hey Hey, My My," only Vedder didn't sing the part of the song Cobain quoted, preferring instead the refrain "There's more to the picture than meets the eye."

The myths surrounding Nirvana—that one must suffer for art and constantly be at war with the mainstream—were dying. Cobain's career, cursed with aggression, had made its last, antagonizing stand, resulting in the most horrifying, needless of casualties, and pop music would be forever changed.

It brought to an end a personal struggle Cobain had been waging with himself from an early age. Once, reflecting on his days as a teenager, he told the *Los Angeles Times* that his father had forced him to sell a guitar and wanted him to join the navy. Military, said Cobain, wasn't an option, but neither was pacifism.

"I took the tests and I guess I scored pretty high because two nights in a row this recruiter came over and tried to get me to sign," Cobain said. "I remember going downstairs trying to decide what I should do with my life and I came to the realization that I'd better go back and get my guitar. To them, I was just wasting my life. To me, I was fighting for it."

Tickets to what would prove to be Nirvana's final show, Terminal 1, Flughafen München-Riem, Munich, Germany, March 1, 1994.

WHAT ELSE COULD I WRITE?
5. THE AFTERMATH
by Mark Yarm

Conundrum Steve: Hey Dave my question for you is, do you think "Grunge" will ever make a comeback? If so what are your thoughts on that?

totallynotdavegrohl: If you mean loud ass guitars, loud ass drums, and screaming ass vocals? That never went away ding dong.

Excerpt from "I Am Dave Grohl: Ask Me Anything" session on Reddit.com, February 9, 2013

For many, the self-inflicted shotgun blast that took the life of Kurt Cobain was the exclamation point at the end of the grunge era. The reality, of course, was not so simple: Grunge didn't go out with a (literal) bang, but with a whimper. And though flannel fashion and teenage angst may have fallen out of favor for a time, grunge never actually died.

After Cobain's suicide, it would take a few years before the major labels purged their rosters of the bulk of the bands they'd signed amid the post-*Nevermind* feeding frenzy—TAD, Mudhoney, the Melvins, the list goes on and on—to make way for the next big thing, or what record execs prayed was the next big thing: electronica, Britpop, pop-punk, nü metal.

"Because we were a grunge band and Kurt was dead and we hadn't hit that kind of success anyway, not only was it an old thing, but we were failures, also-rans," Mudhoney guitarist Steve Turner told me by way of explaining the poor critical and commercial response to the band's 1995 album, *My Brother the Cow*.

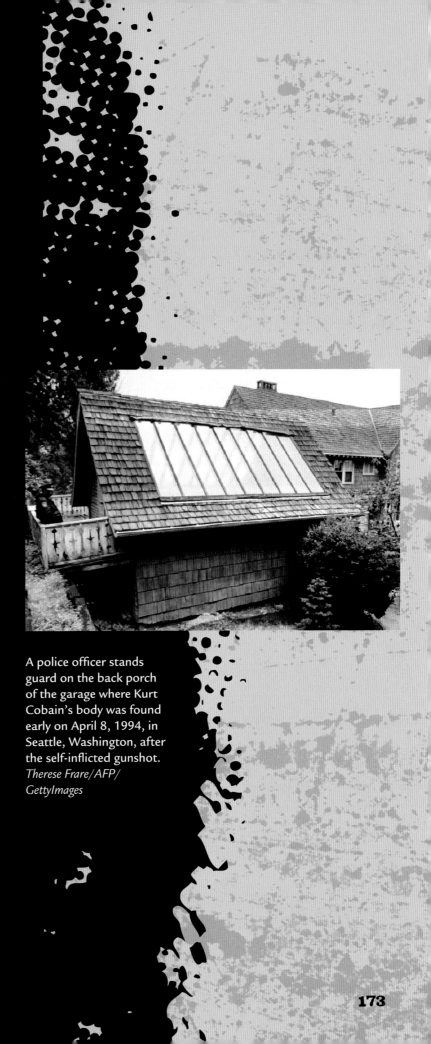

A police officer stands guard on the back porch of the garage where Kurt Cobain's body was found early on April 8, 1994, in Seattle, Washington, after the self-inflicted gunshot. *Therese Frare/AFP/ GettyImages*

Opposite: Kurt Cobain on stage at the Paradiso in Amsterdam, the Netherlands, November 25, 1991. *Peter Pakvis/Redferns/Getty Images*

Nirvana fans burn a poster bearing Kurt Cobain's photograph during a vigil in his memory April 10, 1994, at the Seattle Center, Seattle, Washington.
Therese Frare/AFP/GettyImages

It didn't help Mudhoney's standing with Warner Bros. Records—headed by Nirvana's former manager, Danny Goldberg—that the song "Into Yer Shtik" (with its lyric "Why don't you blow your brains out, too?") was perceived as an attack on Courtney Love.

Still, Mudhoney released one more album on Warner's Reprise label, 1998's *Tomorrow Hit Today*, which was poorly promoted and essentially went nowhere. Today, Mudhoney are back on their original label, Sub Pop, where frontman Mark Arm holds a day job as warehouse manager.

But the grunge backlash didn't affect everyone, or at least not so profoundly. "The backlash didn't touch Soundgarden, it didn't touch Pearl Jam, because they were no longer grunge bands, they were pop bands," argued Mudhoney's onetime A&R rep David

Katznelson. "They had been accepted by a whole other audience." Indeed, the biggest single of Soundgarden's career, the Beatlesque "Black Hole Sun," exploded in the summer of 1994. Aided by a psychedelic, CGI-heavy music video—the furthest thing from the stereotypically downcast and dirty clips of the grunge era—the song peaked at No. 9 on *Billboard*'s Mainstream Top 40.

The passage of time and shifting trends eventually did affect even the most commercially successful grunge acts. By the turn of the century, Britney, *NSYNC, and their teen-pop ilk ruled the airwaves, and only one of the Big Four grunge bands was a functioning concern. Soundgarden had imploded after a particularly stressful 1996–1997 tour behind their album *Superunknown*. Alice in Chains played their last gigs with frontman Layne Staley in the summer of 1996, after which he was largely a recluse, holing up in his Seattle condominium until succumbing to heroin addiction in April 2002. The fact that Staley's body wasn't discovered until two weeks after his death spoke to his utter isolation.

Pearl Jam persisted, but they were nowhere near the commercial powerhouse they once were. The band's sixth album, *Binaural*, released in May 2000, was their first full-length not to go platinum in the United States. (Of course, in the wake of the wild success of their breakout album, Pearl Jam had decided—as a matter of self-preservation—to cease making music videos and pull back on doing press. The band credits these policies, on which they eased up to a degree as years went by, as crucial to the fact that they're still together.)

Which isn't to say that the grunge sound wasn't marketable. The music just got a more populist spin and a prefix appended to its name: post-grunge. Foremost among the post-grunge bands was Creed, a spiritually minded quartet from Tallahassee, Florida, led by muscled singer Scott Stapp, whose baritone singing style owed some (I'm being polite here) to Eddie Vedder's. Creed were critically maligned—and an easy punch line for cooler-than-thou rock fans—but phenomenally successful; their first three albums,

MAREK LIEBERBERG KONZERTAGENTUR AND BLINDFISH PROMOTION PRESENT

IN UTERO

NIRVANA

LIVE '94

SONNTAG, 13. MÄRZ 1994 · 20 UHR
BÖBLINGEN · SPORTHALLE

Poster for cancelled show,
German tour, Spring 1994.

released between 1997 and 2001, went on to sell twenty-three million copies.

Even more popular—and popular to hate—are Nickelback, a Canadian post-grunge juggernaut that's moved more than fifty million units worldwide, espousing the Jäger-swilling, stripper-banging lifestyle pretty much antithetical to everything Nirvana stood for. "I always thought it was strange when these artists like Kurt Cobain or whoever would get really famous and say, 'I don't understand why this is happening to me. I don't understand! Oh, the fame, the fame, the fame!'" Nickelback frontman Chad Kroeger told *Bloomberg Businessweek* in 2012. "There is a mathematical formula to why you got famous."

Unfortunately, there is no mathematical formula for dealing with grief.

"After Kurt's death, I was about as confused as I've ever been," Dave Grohl said in a 1995 press release. "To continue almost seemed in vain. I was always going to be 'that guy from Kurt Cobain's band' and I knew that. I wasn't even sure if I had the desire to make music anymore. I received a postcard from fellow Seattle band 7 Year Bitch, who had also lost a member"—guitarist Stefanie Sargeant, who died of drug-related causes in 1992. "It said, 'We know what you're going through. The desire to play music is gone for now, but it will return. Don't worry.' That fucking letter saved my life, because as much as I missed Kurt, and as much as I felt so lost,

Tickets for cancelled shows, 1994.

I knew that there was only one thing that I was truly cut out to do and that was music."

Six months after Cobain's death, Grohl entered Robert Lang Studios in Seattle to record fifteen songs, the bulk of them written during his time in Nirvana. Grohl sang all the vocal parts and played every instrument—save for a guitar part by Afghan Whigs frontman Greg Dulli—on what ultimately would become the Foo Fighters' 1995 self-titled debut. Once Grohl decided for sure that he wanted to move out from behind the drum kit—he turned down a position as Tom Petty and the Heartbreakers' permanent drummer—he formed an actual band, recruiting the rhythm section of recently disbanded emo heroes Sunny Day Real Estate, and Nirvana's touring guitarist, Pat Smear.

Foo Fighters, a collection of melodic, raw-throated hard rock filled with soaring choruses seemingly designed for stadium sing-alongs, was both a critical and commercial success. The album's first three tracks—"This Is a Call," "I'll Stick Around," and "Big Me"—remain rock-radio staples to this day. "Dave Grohl made his first Foo Fighters album and people were *ecstatic* about that," Turner recalled. "Because they were looking for something to rise from such a tragedy."

Indeed, the Foo Fighters showed that mythological phoenix a thing or two: After more than a decade (and too many lineup changes to detail here), the Foos are one of the most popular arena acts in the world—they easily sold out a two-night stand at Wembley Stadium in 2008—with seven studio albums, eleven Grammys, and more than ten million in sales to their name. Reviewing the Foos' greatest hits album in 2009, *Pitchfork* writer Matthew Perpetua hailed Grohl as "his generation's answer to Tom Petty—a consistent hit machine pumping out working-class rock."

Meanwhile, Grohl has formed a few side projects (most notably the power trio Them Crooked Vultures, with Led Zeppelin's John Paul Jones and Queens of the Stone Age's Josh Homme) and been a promiscuous guest drummer for acts as diverse as Queens of the Stone Age, Killing Joke, Cat Power, and Tenacious D.

Thanks to his sense of humor (the Mentos commercial-spoofing "Big Me" video being just one of many examples) and Everydude charm, Grohl long ago earned the reputation as the Nicest Guy in Rock. He no longer has to worry about merely being "that guy from Kurt Cobain's band"; in fact, the Foos have been around for so long, and become such rock institutions, that some of their younger, more casual listeners are surprised to learn that the band's wide-grinned singer-guitarist once drummed for Nirvana. As if to underscore this transition, in November 2002, the Foo Fighters' "All My Life" bumped Nirvana's long-in-the-vaults track, "You Know You're Right," out of the top spot on the Billboard Modern Rock chart.

Kris Novoselic's post-Nirvana music career, on the other hand, was considerably lower key and less distinguished than that of his friend and former drummer. Grohl had in fact spoken to Novoselic about joining the Foos when he was putting together the band, but with all the Nirvana baggage that would come with such a move, it was deemed not a good idea. "For Krist and I, it would have felt really natural and really great," Grohl told *Rolling Stone* in 1995. "But for everyone else, it would have been weird, and it would have left me in a really bad position. Then I really would have been under the microscope."

Instead, in 1995 Novoselic formed Sweet 75 with Venezuelan-born street singer Yva Las Vegas, a genre-fusing rock project that yielded one largely ignored album, 1997's *Lay Me Down*. In 2002, he teamed with two alt-rock vets—Meat Puppets singer-guitarist Curt Kirkwood and former Sublime drummer Bud Gaugh—to form Eyes Adrift, whose self-titled album unfortunately also was destined for cutout-bin obscurity. In 2006, Novoselic joined a preexisting band, doing a two-year stint as bassist of legendary San Francisco punks Flipper—a key influence on Nirvana. (Cobain famously wore a hand-drawn Flipper T-shirt during Nirvana's 1992 *Saturday Night Live* performance. Twenty years later, the fashion chain Forever 21 introduced a knockoff of Cobain's design, only to pull it amid outcry from Nirvana fans.)

Nirvana's "Pennyroyal Tea" single, also featuring "I Hate Myself and Want to Die" and "Where Did You Sleep Last Night?" (live). It was due to be released as the third single from *In Utero* in April 1994, but after Kurt Cobain's death that month, the planned release was abandoned.

But it was Novoselic's one-off punk band, the No WTO Combo, that spoke to his wider interest in politics and political reform. The Combo, which he put together in late 1999 with Dead Kennedys agit-punk Jello Biafra, Soundgarden guitarist Kim Thayil, and Sweet 75 drummer Gina Mainwal, performed one gig as part of the anti-globalization protests against the World Trade Organization's meeting in Seattle. (A sonic document of that evening, *Live from the Battle in Seattle*, was released on Biafra's Alternative Tentacles label.) Such activism dates back at least as far as Novoselic's days in Nirvana, when he spearheaded benefits for Bosnian rape victims and against Washington State's "erotic music" law, which barred minors from buying recordings deemed "erotic."

In 1995, Novoselic cofounded the Joint Artists and Music Promotions Political Action Committee (JAMPAC), a grassroots organization advocating for artistic freedom of speech, and went on to become a vocal proponent of electoral reform, particularly instant-runoff voting and proportional representation (positions he expounds upon in his 2004 book, *Of Grunge and Government: Let's Fix This Broken Democracy*).

In 2004, he even considered a run for lieutenant governor of Washington, but ultimately decided against it, saying he wanted to stay involved in progressive politics but "the whole thing about running a campaign and being a public servant isn't the way to do it." Today, Novoselic is board chair of the electoral-reform organization FairVote.

"After the end of Nirvana, after the dust settled a little bit, I learned profound lessons on the nature of the human collective," Novoselic said in speeches he delivered during a 1998 grassroots-politics tour of college campuses. "I recognized idolatry as a human attribute that manifests in the structure that we call media. I am struck by the power of the creation of idols, deities, and messiahs, and I'm wary of the structures built around them." It's hard not to assume that he was addressing, at least in part, the cult of worship that, to this day, still surrounds his friend Kurt Cobain.

"I guess that my involvement in politics is a remedy to fretting about idolatry," Novoselic continued. "Discussion and deliberation, consensus then execution is democracy at its best. When it's burdened by ideology and theology, it's at its worst."

Grohl, on the other hand, has indicated that full-time political activism really isn't his thing. "You think being in a rock band is hard?" he told London's Xfm radio in 2005. "Politics is a whole different monster. It's tough—I can't see any of [the Foo Fighters] ever getting involved." However, when they do participate, they go big: the Foo Fighters performed in support of both John Kerry and Barack Obama during their presidential runs, and the Foo's two-song acoustic set during the 2012 DNC had to have been the hippest musical performance ever to grace a major-party national convention.

Despite never-ending gripes about "music these days," the second decade of the twenty-first century

has been a good one for fans of old-school grunge. In late 2011, Pearl Jam celebrated their twentieth anniversary with a two-day festival (featuring Mudhoney, among others) in East Troy, Wisconsin, and released a retrospective documentary directed by Cameron Crowe. In February 2013, Pearl Jam's debut, *Ten*, surpassed the ten million sales mark, and the band has finished their tenth studio album. Meanwhile, after a thirteen-year break, Soundgarden reunited in 2010 and two years later released the ferocious *King Animal*. Alice in Chains roared back in May 2013 with *The Devil Put Dinosaurs Here*, the band's second album with singer William DuVall.

Amid this grunge revival, Nirvana nostalgia became seemingly inescapable: In 2010, news emerged that Grohl and Novoselic had reunited with *Nevermind* producer Butch Vig to record a song for what became the Foos' seventh album, *Wasting Light*. With Vig at the helm, the Foos recorded the entire album in Grohl's

Encino, California, garage using only analog equipment—no Pro Tools here—so as to capture the band's raw sound. Speaking to *Q* magazine, Grohl quipped that the process of working with Vig again was "not unlike going back and fucking a girlfriend you had twenty years ago. It can either be really good or a total fucking disaster."

Fortunately, the chemistry was still there: In April 2011, *Wasting Light* debuted at No. 1 on the *Billboard* Top 200 chart, becoming the first Foos album ever to attain that lofty position. Later that year, the triumvirate of Grohl, Novoselic, and Vig actively promoted the twentieth-anniversary reissues of *Nevermind*, a music-world event that prompted yet another wave of thought pieces on The Album That Changed Everything.

In February 2012, the Foos snared five Grammys, including Best Rock Album, for *Wasting Light*. Accepting that award, Grohl delivered what was without question the speech of the night:

This is a great honor, because this record was a special record for our band. Rather than go to the best studio in the world down the street in Hollywood and rather than use all of the fanciest computers that money can buy, we made this one in my garage with some microphones and a tape machine. . . .

To me this award means a lot because it shows that the human element of music is what's important. Singing into a microphone and learning to play an instrument and learning to do your craft, that's the most important thing for people to do.

It's not about being perfect, it's not about sounding absolutely correct, it's not about what goes on in a computer. It's about what goes on in here [points to heart] and what goes on in here [points to head].

Though his words were clearly heartfelt, Grohl took heat from some critics who interpreted them as a salvo against non-rock music. In response, he issued a clarification declaring his love of "*All* kinds of music," while bewailing the loss of personality in recordings—like "when a song speeds up slightly, or a vocal goes a little sharp"—resulting from the abuse of easy digital "fixes."

Grohl explored the human element of music with his next project, what he called, in an open letter to fans, "my life's most important work": his critically lauded documentary film on Sound City, the dumpy Van Nuys studio where *Nevermind*—as well as albums by Fleetwood Mac, Tom Petty and the Heartbreakers, Neil Young, Rick Springfield, Rage Against the Machine, Nine Inch Nails, Fear, and many others—was recorded. Grohl's directorial debut, *Sound City* is a love letter to the now-defunct studio, its staff and clients, and the machine at its heart, a rare Neve 8028 analog mixing console.

Grohl purchased the Neve when Sound City went under in 2011, reinstalling it in his own Studio 606. The last part of the film documents the soundtrack album that he, the rest of the Foos, and an all-star team of Sound City vets—including Stevie Nicks, Trent Reznor, and Rick Springfield—recorded on the console. Grohl would promote the documentary with a number of performances by the Sound City Players, featuring members of the Foos and a rotating cast of musicians who'd also appeared in the film.

The movie concludes with the weightiest of these collaborations, when Paul McCartney joins Grohl, Novoselic, and Smear in the studio (with Vig behind the console) to hammer out a noisy, new "Helter Skelter"-ish track called "Cut Me Some Slack."

"The fact we were doing that with Paul kept Kris, Pat and I from looking at each other and realizing that, as former members of Nirvana, this hadn't happened in twenty years," Grohl recounted in an interview with British *GQ*. "We were halfway through the day and I looked over at Kris who was bouncing around like he usually does and looked at Pat and he was smiling and beating the shit out of his guitar—wow, it looked like Nirvana. It was a life moment for me."

Everyone involved managed to keep the April 2012 collaboration secret until the day of 12-12-12 The Concert for Sandy Relief, when the foursome debuted "Cut Me Some Slack" to the crowd at Madison Square Garden and millions watching at home on television and the Internet. Predictably, the press touted it as a "Nirvana reunion," although many fans found this heretical, noting that Cobain was irreplaceable, even by a Beatle. (Courtney Love took to the web to express her disdain for the collaboration.)

Grohl and company didn't do anything to counter the "Nirvana reunion" tag. "Nah, I don't care what you call it," Smear told a reporter at *Sound City*'s Sundance premiere. "I'd do it either way." On his blog, Novoselic expressed admiration for the group nickname Sirvana—a reference to McCartney's knighthood—and wrote, "As far as names for the collaboration go, there is no consensus. It's been decided to call it 'The Nirvana Reunion' *and* 'Thee Beatles'—to convey the project is something new and not a nod to musical endeavors past."

Of course, as Novoselic had to have realized that Sirvana couldn't help but be seen as a nod to musical endeavors past. (Indeed, the tone of his post became increasingly tongue-in-cheek.) But, as nostalgic as the *Sound City* film is, it's also a call to arms. As Grohl urged the crowd at the Sundance premiere: "Buy a fucking guitar at a garage sale and start a band with your neighbor. And if everyone is as passionate about this as I am, there will be like a fucking wave of radical garage bands!"

Heed Dave Grohl's words. Grunge is here to stay, ding dong.

Left: One of Kurt Cobain's guitar picks from a Los Angeles show, circa 1989. *Kevin Estrada*
Opposite: A new generation of Nirvana fan: Andrés González Henríquez of Iquique, Chile. *Ricardo "Delonelyman" González*

6. SIGH ETERNALLY
By Andrew Earles

Kim Gordon of Sonic Youth performs "Aneurysm" with Dave Grohl, Krist Novoselic, and Pat Smear (out of frame) at the 29th Annual Rock and Roll Hall of Fame Induction Ceremony at Barclays Center, Brooklyn, New York, on April 10, 2014.
Kevin Mazur/WireImage/Getty Images

"It would be a gross understatement to say a lot has happened since the writing of the first edition . . ."

How many writers have stalled while trying to figure out a clever or original way to communicate the same proclamation when penning new chapters in revised and updated editions? Well, in the case of the Nirvana legacy over the last two to three years, let's just say that sometimes the sheer magnitude of a situation can negate a cliché's baggage.

Over the last several years, in a situation not likely to reverse any time soon, Nirvana's legacy has maintained a more conspicuous profile than that of any classically considered legends in the entire history of rock (including the Beatles). The past thirty-five years have seen no band in the overarching genre of rock, whether posthumous or active, exact an influence on music and culture that even comes close to touching Nirvana's.

Metallica? Unless we're talking about an influence on the increased use of sarcasm and derogatory commentary toward a band, the verdict is that Nirvana's footprint on everything rock-related has lapped the Rolling Stones of metal. Repeatedly.

Conversely, there's a negative side to all of this, and while this may seem like the ultimate in stating the obvious, it's not that simple. Never has a rock band's past been so retroactively distorted into an irreversible fiction by incessant mythologizing, conjecture, wild speculation, and romanticizing rhetoric. The Cobain biographical narrative—specifically in regard to the culturally irresponsible mishandling of subjects such as drug abuse, depression, and suicide—is now impenetrable with inaccurate and overcooked connectivity between that which is completely unrelated, too chronologically disparate, or just plain untrue. But to veer back into the realm of music—the reason we're all here anyway—the latter halves of 2015

In Utero engineer Steve Albini oversaw the album's "2013 Mix," which he described to podcaster Vish Khanna as a snapshot of the songs "from a different angle." Grohl, Novoselic, and Smear provided input. The year 2013 also saw the re-release of *In Utero* in "deluxe" and "super deluxe" editions. *Voyageur Press collection*

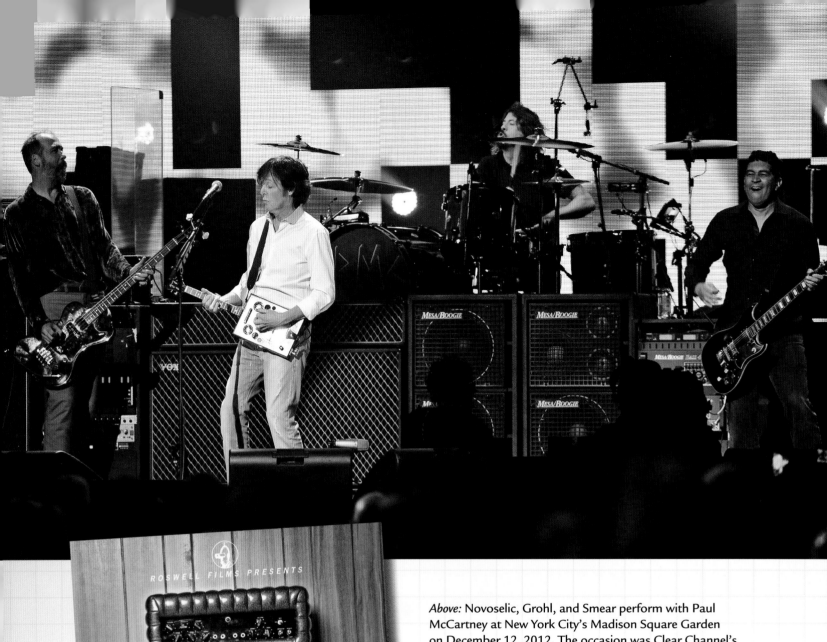

Above: Novoselic, Grohl, and Smear perform with Paul McCartney at New York City's Madison Square Garden on December 12, 2012. The occasion was Clear Channel's "12-12-12" benefit for the Robin Hood Relief Fund to aid victims of Hurricane Sandy. The performance blossomed into a 2013 concert appearance in Seattle and a 2014 Grammy for Best Rock Song, "Cut Me Some Slack." *Larry Busacca/Getty Images for Clear Channel*

Left: Grohl's documentary about the Van Nuys, California, studio where *Nevermind* and dozens of other legendary albums were recorded brought out many notable talking heads—as well as critical accolades. *Voyageur Press collection*

Opposite: Grohl performs with former Creedence Clearwater Revival frontman John Fogerty during the Pre-Grammy Gala and Salute at the Beverly Hilton in Beverly Hills, California, on January 25, 2014. Fogerty was one of dozens of rockers who appeared in Grohl's *Sound City* documentary released the previous year. *Larry Busacca/Getty Images for NARAS*

ROSWELL FILMS PRESENTS

SOUND CITY

DIRECTED BY
DAVE GROHL

and 2013 added a great deal of previously unheard music to the band's and Cobain's bodies of work, though the two releases in question were otherwise totally different where quality and cultural necessity are concerned.

In early to mid-2013, word began spreading about an upcoming reissue campaign set to coincide with the twentieth anniversary of *In Utero*'s release on September 13. The "super deluxe" version of the reissue made available a mind-blowing amount of material that had never entered the public arena. Unlike many cases of typically overindulgent and filler-saturated treatments of past albums, this situation served as one big historically corrective measure on a couple of levels.

Ideally, any out-of-touch notions that the album's overall nature and delivery harmed Nirvana's legacy could finally be put to bed. *In Utero* is the only Nirvana full-length that managed to traverse the last two decades without any element of datedness and remains by far the most influential album in the band's discography when it comes to forward-thinking guitar-oriented acts formed since its release.

In addition, the perennial and totally undeserved pariah of the *In Utero* saga, engineer Steve Albini, was brought in to handle the remastering and remixing duties with Dave Grohl and Krist Novoselic sitting in at Electrical Audio Studios, which Albini designed and built in the mid-1990s and operates to this day. (Albini's

Grohl accepts his statue during Nirvana's induction at the 29th Annual Rock and Roll Hall of Fame Induction Ceremony, Brooklyn, New York, April 10, 2014. Pictured from left: Novoselic and Grohl; Cobain's sister Kimberly Cobain; his mother, Wendy O'Connor; and sister Breanne O'Connor; Courtney Love; and Michael Stipe, who inducted the band. *Jeff Kravitz/FilmMagic/Getty Images*
Opposite: Novoselic and Grohl at the 29th Annual Rock and Roll Hall of Fame Induction Ceremony. *Dimitrios Kambouris (Novoselic) and Kevin Mazur (Grohl) both WireImage/Getty Images*

192

original mix, as it left Pachyderm Studios with Nirvana, before Scott Litt's polishing job, was made available as a standalone Record Store Day release.)

The super deluxe version of *In Utero* features a mind-blowing mountain of bonus material: a whopping seventy songs plus MTV's 1993 *Live & Loud* concert DVD and, most notably, a reprint of Albini's four-page work-and-recording proposal that the engineer faxed to the band in 1992 (a highly recommended read). On the Kreative Kontrol podcast in August 2013, Albini gave an extensive, honest, and very revealing behind-the-scenes account of *In Utero*'s recording, revealing information

that had never been disclosed in relation to the conjecture-ridden saga. In the podcast, Albini claimed that rereading the letter was cringe-inducing but that it put the entire situation into proper perspective—something that was long overdue.

In stark contrast (on every level) to the *In Utero* re-release was the much-hyped late-2015 release of *Montage of Heck: The Home Recordings*. Curated by *Montage of Heck* director Brett Morgen (who admitted to harboring a complete unfamiliarity with Nirvana or Cobain before he was approached by Courtney Love in 2007 about making the documentary) from the lot of spoken journal and practice cassettes that were also edited into much of the film documentary, *The Home Recordings* were talked up throughout the year as an upcoming Kurt Cobain "solo album," perhaps giving the misrepresentation that the recordings were a lost studio

Joan Jett and Novoselic during the performance of "Smells Like Teen Spirit" at the 29th Annual Rock and Roll Hall of Fame Induction Ceremony, Brooklyn, New York, April 10, 2014. *Kevin Mazur/WireImage/Getty Images*

Right: Grohl practices backstage with Bruce Springsteen and Zac Brown prior to the Concert for Valor on the National Mall in Washington, D.C., on November 11, 2014. Controversially, the three covered Creedence Clearwater Revival's antiwar song, "Fortunate Son," at the event. *Kevin Mazur/Getty Images for HBO*
Below: Grohl also performed "My Hero" and "Everlong." *Jeff Kravitz/Getty Images for HBO*

album. Staggered preview material, including a home-recorded demo of "Been a Son" and "Sappy" released in promotion of the thirty-one-track collection, gave the illusion that more fully realized material would be included.

Instead, and unlike the documentary, the reality of *Montage of Heck: The Home Recordings* was best summed up by its critical reception. Greg Kot (who also wrote the *In Utero* essay in this book), in his piece about the recordings titled "Cobain's Awful Aftermath Is a Mess" for the *Chicago Tribune*, wrote: "Munchkin voices, yodeling, a meditation on sea monkeys and Paula Abdul, distracted guitar playing, a phone call for his girlfriend that interrupts a 'recording session'—if that sounds compelling, Kurt Cobain's 'Montage of Heck—

The Home Recordings' (Universal) is for you."

Kot continued:

By presenting Cobain in this vulnerable setting—alone, unedited and unscrutinized, his mind wandering where it will—"The Home Recordings" aims to illuminate process, the missing link between inspiration and finished recording. Cobain, Nirvana's singer and guitarist, killed himself in 1994 at age 27, leaving behind a small but influential body of work that decades later continues to fascinate, influence and sell.

And selling seems to be the sole reason for this collection of scraps to exist. It quickly becomes apparent that most of these low-fi

Opposite: Zakk Wylde, Grohl, Lemmy Kilmister, Taylor Hawkins, and Slash perform Chuck Berry's "Let It Rock" during Grohl's birthday bash at the Forum on January 10, 2015, in Inglewood, California. What began as a last-minute Foo Fighters gig turned into an all-star affair featuring, among others, Paul Stanley, David Lee Roth, Perry Farrell, and Alice Cooper. *Kevin Mazur/WireImage*
Below: Foo Fighters Chris Shiflett, Nate Mendel, Dave Grohl, Pat Smear, and Taylor Hawkins promote *Sonic Highways* with Chelsea Handler (top row) at the iHeartRadio Theater in Burbank, California, on March 17, 2015. *Kevin Winter/Getty Images for iHeartMedia*

All Voyageur Press collection

recordings are just Cobain goofing and daydreaming, distractedly playing his guitar and breaking into strange voices for his own amusement while sitting on the couch and watching TV (his preferred work method, as he stated in several interviews).

Audra Schroeder of the *Daily Dot* wrote in her piece titled "The Disturbing Commodification of Kurt Cobain's Home Recordings":

Yes, you're right to feel icky about that echoing ca-ching. Much of *Montage of Heck* [the documentary] feels a little too intimate: the home videos of Kurt and Courtney; Cobain nodding off while holding daughter Frances Bean. It's hard to imagine an audience that would want to shell out anywhere from $17 to $130 (!) on tracks that are essentially works in progress, stop-start songs: During "Burn the Rain," Cobain stops playing to answer the phone and take a message

for his then-girlfriend, Tracy Marander, and then the tape cuts off. Opener "The Yodel Song" is a typical Nirvana chord progression with aimless yodeling over it. "Aberdeen," which is used to great effect in the doc, is a spoken word account of Cobain's first sexual experience and a subsequent suicide attempt, but one wonders if Cobain wanted anyone to hear it.

These are not voices in the wilderness. *Montage of Heck: The Home Recordings* was met with a chorus of fan and critical dissent about the undeniably exploitative and crassly opportunistic nature of the endeavor. The recordings and documentary, for better or worse, exponentially increased the amount of biographically revelatory Nirvana/Cobain historical information and content.

And so did *Soaked in Bleach*.

Regardless of where one might stand on the circumstances surrounding Cobain's death, Benjamin Statler's *Soaked in Bleach* docudrama is surprisingly

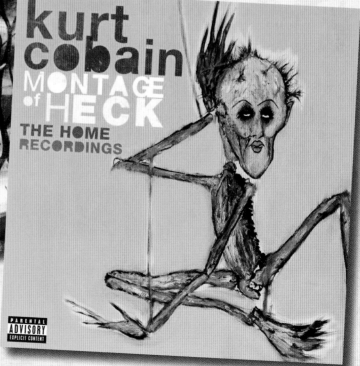

Opposite: Frances Bean Cobain attends the *Kurt Cobain: Montage of Heck* premiere at the Egyptian Theatre in Hollywood, April 21, 2015. *Jeff Kravitz/FilmMagic/Getty Images* *Below:* The *Montage of Heck* soundtrack album and deluxe edition. The releases were met with much critical indifference. *Voyageur Press collection*

powerful and engaging. Immediately written off by major media outlets as a conspiracy-kook throwaway (with some writers who expressed this opinion actually admitting their refusal to watch it), *Soaked in Bleach* was a provocative, disturbing, and all-around excellent true-crime docudrama. Courtney Love raised eyebrows when she attempted to serve cease-and-desist orders to theaters showing an initial run of the film in 2015, but as the year drew to a close, the film went on to garner much more respect. (The film was picked up by Netflix in September 2015.)

One of the more chilling and memorable moments in *Soaked in Bleach* has former Seattle Police Chief Norm Stamper commenting:

> We should in fact have taken steps to study patterns involved in the behavior of key individuals who had a motive to see Kurt Cobain dead. If in fact Kurt Cobain was murdered, as opposed to having committed suicide, and it was possible to learn that, shame on us for not doing that. That was in fact our responsibility. It's about right and wrong. It's about honor. It's about ethics. If we didn't get it right the first time, we damn well better get it right the second time, and I would tell you right now if I were the chief of police, I would reopen this investigation.

In fact, in April 2014, the twentieth anniversary of Cobain's death, the Seattle Police Department had "reopened" the investigation into Cobain's death but closed it (or reclosed it) a week or so later, sticking to the original "suicide" ruling. The police added no new information other than a few previously unreleased death-scene photos to appease public pressure amid media observation of the anniversary. Most of that observation took place under the guise of a celebration of Cobain's legacy, though there were lapses in taste, notably a hoax announcement that a Cobain holograph would lead the reformed Nirvana at that year's Coachella.

Rather than a holographic Cobain, St. Vincent ("Lithium"), Lorde ("All Apologies"), Joan Jett ("Smells Like Teen Spirit"), and Sonic Youth's Kim Gordon ("Aneurysm") stood in for the singer on April 10, performing Nirvana staples for the band's induction

Above: Director Benjamin Statler's *Soaked in Bleach* was a surprisingly powerful and engaging "docudrama." *Voyageur Press collection*

Opposite: The Foo Fighters served as the last ever musical guests on the *Late Show with David Letterman* on May 20, 2015, at the Ed Sullivan Theater in New York. The legendary host was a self-proclaimed "Fighters of Foo" fan ever since giving the band their first TV appearance in 1995. *John Paul Filo/CBS via Getty Image*

into the Rock and Roll Hall of Fame. Prior to the performances, the band was formally inducted by R.E.M.'s Michael Stipe, after which Dave Grohl gave what might be one of the best speeches in the history of the event. Offering a roll call of the drummers who preceded him in the band, Grohl made sure that Chad Channing, who was in the audience, got due credit, especially for his contributions to the band's body of work.

Then, in the small hours of April 11, all of those guest vocalists (minus Lorde) joined Grohl, Novoselic, and

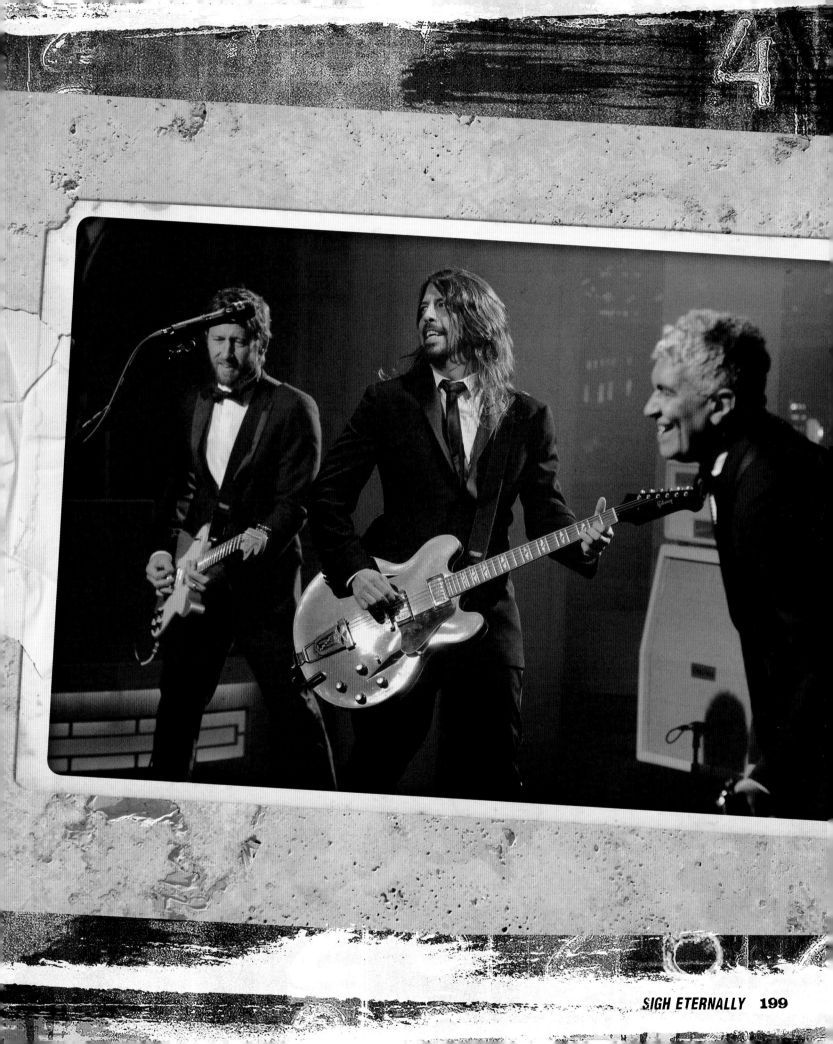

Smear for an invite-only show (it was reported that some in the audience paid $10,000 to attend) at Brooklyn's premier underground metal venue, the just-over-two-hundred-capacity St. Vitus Bar. Joining the guest front-women from earlier in the evening were Dinosaur Jr's J Mascis and John McCauley of Deer Tick, who are known to play Nirvana covers shows as Deervana.

Nirvana's music has never stopped influencing underground guitar bands, and their discography has outlasted the meaningless term "grunge," coined as a marketing tool used everywhere from small local music scenes to Fashion Week 1992. Somehow, grunge lived on as a subgenre and musical style that really did not exist after 1992, if it ever did at all.

Great examples of Nirvana's vital influence on a cross-section of today's vanguard of guitar-driven indie rock, noise rock, and cerebrally metallic bands can be heard on two tribute albums released on Record Store Day in 2014 and 2015 by the excellent Robotic Empire label. The artists featured on 2014's amazing *In Utero: In Tribute* include Thursday, Circa Survive, Jay Reatard, Ceremony, Whirr, Young Widows, Thou, Pygmy Lush, and These Arms Are Snakes; on 2015's *Whatever Nevermind* album, the most musically and culturally influential album of the last forty years is tackled by Kylesa, Torche, Boris, La Dispute, Cave In, Touché Amoré, Wrong, and Nothing.

Nirvana's post-1994 legacy is trumped by an unimpeachable fact about the music Kurt Cobain made for a future in which he wouldn't participate: new Nirvana fans are minted by the minute. Those who choose to let music dictate their paths through life to some degree would be hard-pressed to find a better modern rock discography to soundtrack "life-altering" moments and serve as a gateway to the band's lesser known influences, more challenging underground fare, and the bands that were influenced *by* Nirvana. For decades, music lifers have carried Led Zeppelin, Black Sabbath, the Velvet Underground, or others as go-to references. Add Nirvana to that list.

Grohl performs with the Foo Fighters at the Carisport of Cesena, Italy, on November 3, 2015. He had the throne constructed after breaking his leg at a concert in Gothenburg, Sweden, on June 12, 2015 (he finished the show). *Paul Bergen/Red Ferns via Getty Images*

CONTRIBUTORS

Jay Blakesberg (www.blakesberg.com) is a San Francisco–based commercial photographer and filmmaker whose work appears regularly in many magazines, including *Rolling Stone* and *Guitar Player*. Over the last thirty-plus years his photographic rock 'n' roll journey has seen him work with legendary artists like the Grateful Dead, Carlos Santana, Tom Waits, Neil Young, Nirvana, Soundgarden, Radiohead, Phish, Dave Matthews, and John Lee Hooker, to name just a few. He has published several volumes of his work, including illustrated books on the Grateful Dead, Primus, the Mother Hips, and the Flaming Lips, as well as a retrospective of his music photography titled *Traveling on a High Frequency*. Blakesberg has also directed live concert video for the Flaming Lips, Spearhead, Gov't Mule, Jackie Greene, Widespread Panic, and the Allman Brothers. In 2011 he began working with the estate of legendary music photographer Jim Marshall, handling domestic licensing of Marshall's epic body of work.

Charles R. Cross (www.charlesrcross.com) is the author of seven books, including bestselling biographies of Kurt Cobain and Jimi Hendrix. Cross was editor of *The Rocket* from 1986 through 2000, and chronicled the rise of the Northwest scene during the heyday of grunge. He has written for hundreds of newspapers and magazines, from *Rolling Stone* to the London *Times*. He lectures at a number of colleges on journalism and pop culture and lives near Seattle.

Jim DeRogatis (www.jimdero.com) is a lecturer at Columbia College Chicago. He has written nine books about music, continues to critique new sounds on his blog at WBEZ.org, and with Greg Kot co-hosts *Sound Opinions,* "the world's only rock 'n' roll talk show," which can be heard nationally on public radio or on podcast at www.soundopinions.org.

Guitar World contributing writer **Alan di Perna** is a left-handed guitarist and author of *Guitar Masters: Intimate Portraits* and *Green Day: The Ultimate Unauthorized History*, among other books.

Andrew Earles is from Memphis, Tennessee, where he writes for Spin.com, *Magnet, The Memphis Flyer, Vice,* and other print and online outlets. His first book, *Hüsker Dü: The Story of the Noise-Pop Pioneers Who Launched Modern Rock*, was published by Voyageur Press in November 2010, and he has contributed to other Voyageur books about AC/DC, Rush, Led Zeppelin, and Queen. His Jay Reatard obituary for Spin.com was selected as an honorable mention in Da Capo's *Best Music Writing 2011*. He is also the author of Voyageur Press's *Gimme Indie Rock*.

Kevin Estrada (www.kevinestrada.com) was a preteen when he began his photo career by smuggling his camera into some of the most legendary concerts in Los Angeles. For the last thirty-plus years he has photographed countless musicians in concert, backstage, on the road, and in the studio. He continues to make his living as a rock 'n' roll photographer and music video director in the L.A. area.

Gillian G. Gaar first typed the name "Nirvana" in March 1988 when she was calendar editor at *The Rocket* magazine in Seattle. Since then, she has written four books about the band, including *Entertain Us: The Rise of Nirvana*, and was also project consultant for Nirvana's *With the Lights Out* box set. She has also written books about Elvis, Green Day, and Bruce Springsteen, as well as *She's a Rebel: The History of Women in Rock & Roll*. She lives in Seattle.

Bob Gendron writes for *TONEAudio* and is a regular contributor to the *Chicago Tribune* and *DownBeat*. He wrote Continuum's 33 1/3 book on the Afghan Whigs' *Gentlemen*, and his work has appeared in numerous other publications. A Chicago native, Gendron worked in an indie record store during Nirvana's Sub Pop and initial Geffen tenures. He plays hockey, roots for the Blackhawks and White Sox, has a weakness for craft beer, and loves cold weather.

Greg Kot (www.gregkot.com) has been the music critic at the *Chicago Tribune* since 1990. With Jim DeRogatis, he co-hosts the nationally syndicated rock 'n' roll talk show *Sound Opinions*. Kot's books include *I'll Take You There: Mavis Staples, the Staple Singers and the March up Freedom's Highway*, as well as *Wilco: Learning How to Die*, and *Ripped: How the Wired Generation Revolutionized Music*. He also coauthored *The Beatles vs. The Rolling Stones: Sound Opinions on the Great Rock 'n' Roll Rivalry* with DeRogatis. Kot lives in Chicago.

Todd Martens has covered music and video games for the *Los Angeles Times* since mid-2007. Previously, Martens reported on the music business for *Billboard*. His first paid writing gig was for the defunct 'zine *Punk Planet*. He continues to torture himself by stubbornly rooting for the Chicago Cubs, and one of his biggest regrets in life is giving away his ticket to Nirvana's *In Utero* tour in favor of finishing a high school book report on *The Canterbury Tales*.

Charles Peterson is best known for his documentation of the music phenomenon known as "grunge," culminating with his critically acclaimed monograph *Touch Me I'm Sick* (2003). Peterson's photographs have graced hundreds of record covers and appeared in publications worldwide including the *Village Voice*, *NME*, the *New York Times*, *Mojo*, *People*, *Rolling Stone*, *Spin*, *Entertainment Weekly*, *Guitar World*, and *Newsweek*. His other previous monographs include *Screaming Life* (1995) and *Pearl Jam: Place/Date* (1997). His photographs are featured in the permanent collection of Seattle's Experience Music Project (EMP).

Mark Yarm (@markyarm) is the author of *Everybody Loves Our Town: An Oral History of Grunge*, a *Time* magazine book of the year. A former senior editor at *Blender* magazine, Yarm has written for *Wired*, *Rolling Stone*, *Spin*, *Esquire*, *Men's Health,* and numerous other publications, and regularly blogs about grunge at www.grungebook.tumblr.com. He lives in Brooklyn and is of no relation to Mudhoney singer Mark Arm.

INDEX

A

Albini, Steve, 138, 140–141, 152, 160, 163–164, 187, 189
Alice in Chains, 77, 174, 181
Anderson, Dawn, 39–40
Arcade Fire, 142
Azerrad, Michael, 57, 65, 92, 94, 109, 121

B

Babior, Greg, 51, 70
Bayer, Samuel, 104
Beatles, The, 187
Black, Lori, 17
Black Sabbath, 200
Brown, Zac, 193
Burckhard, Aaron, 18, 29
Butthole Surfers, 39, 95

C

Channing, Chad, 22, 31, 34, 37, 40, 43, 48, 52, 57, 64–65, 87–88, 92, 198
Clash, the, 99–100, 146
Cobain, Frances Bean, 132, 147, 165, 168
Cobain, Kurt, 12, 31, 33–34, 37, 41, 43, 46, 52, 57, 59, 63–65, 70–72, 74–75, 84, 87, 90–95, 97–98, 104–105, 109, 115, 120–122, 132, 134, 136, 141–142, 145, 149–151, 160–163, 166, 181–182, 189, 191
    appearance on MTV's *Headbanger's Ball*, 126
    death, 11, 137–138, 143, 168, 171, 173, 176
    drug use and health problems, 55, 60, 121, 131, 164–165, 168
    early years of Nirvana, 18–27, 29
    first band, 17
    first recordings, 16
    guitars he used, 23, 50, 60, 74, 135, 154–159
    incident with Axl Rose, 147–148
    inclusion of his image in *Guitar Hero*, 137–138, 142
    internal conflict about being a rock star and "selling out," 99, 121, 128, 138 141, 145, 175
    Journals, 12, 94, 141
    life growing up, 12–14
    living in Seattle, 11
    on wannabe alternative bands, 96
    personal top 50 albums, 12–13, 15–16, 19, 22–25, 30, 32, 34, 37, 48, 51, 56, 60, 63, 68, 70, 74, 77, 84, 89, 91, 97, 100, 106, 110, 117, 119, 121, 126, 131, 138, 142, 145–146, 148, 151–152, 161, 163, 166–167, 169–171
Codeine, 134
Crover, Dale, 16, 18, 21, 29, 31, 33, 39, 43

D

Deervana, 200
Dinosaur Jr, 77, 88, 95, 106, 113

E

Endino, Jack, 21, 24–25, 29–31, 33, 39–40, 59
Estrada, Kevin, 91
Eugenics, 96
Everman, Jason, 40, 43, 55, 57

F

Fecal Matter, 17–18, 30
Fisk, Steve, 59
Flaming Lips, 95
Flipper, 138, 177
Fluid, 96
Fogerty, John, 188–189
Foo Fighters, 195, 198–199, 201
Foster, Dave, 21, 30, 33–34

INDEX

© 2022 Quarto Publishing Group USA Inc.

NEW TEXT © 2016 Quarto Publishing Group

This edition published in 2022 by Chartwell Books,
an imprint of The Quarto Group
142 West 36th Street, 4th Floor
New York, NY 10018 USA

T (212) 779-4972 F (212) 779-6058
www.Quarto.com

First published in 2013 by Voyageur Press,
an imprint of The Quarto Group
100 Cummings Center Suite 265D,
Beverly, MA 01915 USA.

T (612) 344-8100 F (612) 344-8692
www.Quarto.com

10 9 8 7 6 5 4 3 2 1

Chartwell titles are also available at discount for retail, wholesale, promotional, and bulk purchase. For details, contact the Special Sales Manager by email at specialsales@quarto.com or by mail at The Quarto Group, Attn: Special Sales Manager, 100 Cummings Center, Suite 265D, Beverly, MA 01915, USA.

ISBN: 978-0-7858-4179-1

Acquiring Editors: Dennis Pernu and Michael Dregni
Project Manager: Alyssa Bluhm
Art Director: James Kegley
Layout: Simon LarkinPrinted in China

ON THE FRONT COVER: Paul Bergen/Getty Images
ON THE BACK COVER: Black and white photo: Michael Linssen/Getty Images
Full color band photo: Jeff Kravitz/Getty Images
PAGE 3: São Paulo, Brazil, November 1, 1993. Joe Giron/Corbis
TITLE PAGE: Frankfurt, Germany, November 12, 1991. Paul Bergen/Redferns/Getty Images
PAGE 8: Playing hide-and-seek. Pictorial Press Ltd/AlamyImage credits: Shutterstock

Printed in China